New Brunswick
UNDER WATER
The 2018 Saint John River Flood

Lisa Hrabluk
Photo editor: Michael Hawkins

Copyright 2018 Lisa Hrabluk

All rights reserved. No part of this book covered by the copyrights hereon may be reproduced or used in any form or by any means – graphic, electronic, or mechanical – without the prior written permission of the publisher. Any request for photocopying, recording, taping, or information storage and retrieval systems of any part of this book shall be directed in writing to the Canadian Reprography Collective, 379 Adelaide Street, West, Suite M1, Toronto, Ontario, M5V 1S5.

MacIntyre Purcell Publishing Inc.
194 Hospital Rd.
Lunenburg, Nova Scotia
B0J 2C0
(902) 640-3350

www.macintyrepurcell.com
info@macintyrepurcell.com

Printed and bound in Canada by Friesens

Design and layout: Denis Cunningham
Cover design: Denis Cunningham
Cover photo: Andrew Vaughn, Canadian Press

ISBN: 978-1-77276-115-3

Library and Archives Canada Cataloguing in Publication

Hrabluk, Lisa, author
    Mighty river : the 2018 New Brunswick flood / Lisa Hrabluk ; photo editor, Michael Hawkins.

ISBN 978-1-77276-115-3 (softcover)

    1. Floods--New Brunswick. 2. Floods--New Brunswick--Pictorial works. 3. Saint John River (Me. and N.B.). 4. Saint John River (Me. and N.B.)--Pictorial works. I. Title.

GB1399.5.C3H73 2018   551.48'9097153   C2018-903491-2

MacIntyre Purcell Publishing Inc. would like to acknowledge the financial support of the Government of Canada and the Nova Scotia Department of Tourism, Culture and Heritage.

TABLE OF CONTENTS

BAROMETER FALLING
The spring freshet arrives in New Brunswick like clockwork each year, rising during the last week of April and departing in early May. At least, that's how it's supposed to work. The flood of 2018 was different 7

RIVER PEOPLE
The Saint John River is arguably the most historically and culturally significant river in Canada. It is the second largest watershed east of the Mississippi River, surpassed only by the St. Lawrence River 17

A RIVER ON THE RISE
On April 23, New Brunswick Emergency Measures Organization issued its first flood advisory. Two days later, on April 25, River Watch issued another advisory: much of the Saint John River would reach flood stage in the coming days. The flood had arrived 29

WATERSHED DOWN
By Tuesday, May 1, New Brunswickers woke up to the news of widespread closures, detours and warnings. Three river ferries had service suspended while about 800 homes in Saint John were in immediate danger of flooding. Emergency shelters were set up and sandbagging stations were established. And the winds came............. 41

COTTAGE LIFE
For cottagers, Mother's Day weekend normally represents the start of their favourite season. It's time to open the cottage, reconnect with neighbours and get ready for another summer at the lake. Instead, many families spent the next couple of weeks surveying the damage and trying to figure out what would come next 55

ANGER AND LOSS
The 2018 flood didn't behave like other floods. Amid the stress and sadness of the flood's aftermath, few people had much praise for the government's slow speed of delivery and lack of timely information about help to repair damage sustained in the high water 65

FORECASTING THE FLOOD
The challenge in 2018 was the amount of water in the snow. Normally, as snow melts, it absorbs part of the melt back into itself. This year, the weather fluctuated up north causing the snow to melt, freeze, get absorbed back in the snow. Then it rained far more than forecasters had predicted 79

EMERGENCY CREWS AT WORK
When the old timers started coming out, that's when Chief Jody Price knew the flood of 2018 was like no other flood before it 87

HELPING HANDS
With their only access road flooded, Darlings Island residents had two choices: either seek temporary shelter off the island or wade or paddle your way across the one-kilometre stretch to the mainland 95

BUILD BACK BETTER
The people who reside along the river now understand they will need to develop strategies and be more resilient in dealing with an increasing number of intense weather events in the future 105

COMMUNITIES ON THE RISE
Almost every New Brunswicker has a relationship with water but one of the biggest challenges people have is a complete misunderstanding of what it means to be a steward of it 113

From the Author

Writing this book was a gift and a privilege and I am grateful for the patience and assistance I received from numerous people as I worked on this project through the summer of 2018.

First and most importantly, to the residents of New Brunswick who so generously shared their stories about the 2018 flood, reaching out to me via social media and emails to send in their photos and to offer to meet up for a coffee. I am particularly indebted to Markus Harvey, Cecelia Brooks and Ron Tremblay who were generous with their time, answering follow-up questions and connecting me with others.

Within the Government of New Brunswick, Geoffrey McCann, Jasmin Boisvert and Darwin Curtis and NB Power's Patrick Lacroix tracked down statistics and information for me that were essential to telling the science and engineering story.

I am grateful to John MacIntyre and Vernon Oickle of MacIntyre Purcell Publishing Inc. for offering me the opportunity to tell this important story and also for the chance to co-create it with my husband, Michael Hawkins. While Michael and I toured the flood zone together, we were fortunate to have our 'home team', the parents of our daughter's softball team, the KV Dynamites, looking after Alex when we were on the road or writing. In particular, Thaddee and Sylvie Bourque who fed her, got her to practices and to games.

Finally, we are thankful for Alex Hawkins, for her patience, support, love and cheerleading during the telling of this story.

— Lisa Hrabluk

(Ben Sandwith photo)

BAROMETER FALLING

(Opposite) Drone photos show the incredibly high waters that swallowed the downtown Fredericton waterfront, including the Crowne Plaza-Lord Beaverbrook Hotel parking lot.

The spring freshet, or flood, has been a regular part of life for everyone who has called the river home for thousands of years. Both Indigenous oral knowledge and scientific exploration reach back more than 12 thousand years and the earliest written records note an unusually high freshet in 1696.

The spring flood arrives like clockwork each year, rising during the last week of April and departing in early May. At least, that's how it's supposed to work.

The flood of 2018 was different. This year the flood came fast — faster than anyone could ever remember. Strong currents and even stronger winds broke through doors, ripped holes in roofs and tore cottages, docks and sheds from moorings. It came fast and furious and was not eager to leave.

HIGHER GROUND

Water was sloshing about in the parking lot of the Crown Plaza Fredericton-Lord Beaverbrook Hotel as Cecelia Brooks, scientist and Indigenous knowledge expert (made her way inside.)

She was there to meet with colleagues and as they all gathered in a conference room overlooking the river, there was only one thing everyone wanted to talk about: THE FLOOD.

Life was just beginning to return to normal in downtown Fredericton, which had been all but shut down as the Saint John River (known to the Wolastoqiyik [Maliseet] which means "Beautiful River") had barrelled over its banks, flooding everything in its path.

(Left) Flooding in downtown Fredericton surrounds Chancery Place, a Government of New Brunswick office building that houses the Premier's Office.

As Brooks listened to her colleagues' stories, she looked through the conference-room window to the north side of Fredericton. "Do you notice the old reserve at St. Mary's?" she said to them, pointing to a green space on the opposite bank of the river at the foot of Union Street. "It isn't flooded."

For Brooks, it was an illustration of how Indigenous knowledge, drawn from generations of keen observation and storytelling, can provide guidance to contemporary science as New Brunswick residents learn to live with extreme weather events, such as the 2018 flood. "We didn't camp there on a whim," she said. "We knew that wouldn't flood."

WARNING SIGNS

Fourteen kilometres downriver from Brooks and her colleagues at the Crown Plaza, Markus Harvey stood on his front porch, exhausted. A lifelong resident of Maugerville, Harvey, like Brooks, knew to listen to the river. It's why he and many of his neighbours had built their homes above the level of the last historic flood, which occurred in 1973 and reached 2.17 metres (7.11 feet) above sea level.

(Above) The Big Potato, a Maugerville landmark on Route 105, was quickly surrounded by the river.

Both Maugerville and neighbouring Sheffield are rural communities located on a low-lying bend on the northeast side of the river across from Oromocto. Residents know to expect some flooding during the spring freshet and they watch for the warning signs — heavy snow up north, late April rains and warming temperatures — to gauge how and when to prepare.

But nothing could really prepare them for this.

On May 4, the river reached 1973 levels. And it was still rising. Harvey leaned against a porch beam and looked up and down the river. Highway 105, which runs between his home and the riverbank had disappeared, the yellow lines faintly visible beneath the water.

RIVER BECOMES A LAKE

No matter where he looked there was water. His beloved river had become a lake and converted his home — and the homes, barns and storefronts of family and neighbours — into water-logged islands.

A gregarious storyteller, Harvey is known as the unofficial mayor of Maugerville and each year during the spring freshet he writes regularly on the Maugerville Flood Watch Facebook page to keep people informed. Normally self-effacing and chipper online, on May 4 Harvey's tone turned serious as he considered the long, expensive and emotionally painful recovery he and his neighbours faced.

"I'm going on day 5 without power, surrounded by water with a basement full of sewer back-up and empty gas tanks for my generator," he wrote. "I'm in the middle of this and know this is going to be an expensive out of pocket cost for us to get back some sense of normal and get our families home."

(Right) The eerie beauty of the flooded river in Maugerville, where floodwaters reached the highest.

(Below) A Canadian flag flaps in the breeze as residents of Grand Lake surveyed the damage caused by the 2018 flood.

(Jon McEachern photo)

(Markus Harvey photo)

(Markus Harvey photo)

(Opposite) Buzz Harvey drives the tractor while Tej, Ji and Chazan Harvey ride along on the back as they prepare to deliver sandbags during the first weekend of the flood.

(Right) Volunteers shovel sand in Grand Bay-Westfield at the site affectionately nicknamed The Pit, located at Keel Construction's property, all of the sand donated by the Hobart family.

SANDBAGGING

Chris Taylor was one of the many volunteers to reach out to New Brunswickers who needed help.

On the morning of May 4, Taylor had hoped to get a few precious hours of sleep before heading back out to join one of the sandbagging details that was working to keep the water at bay in the Saint John region. Instead she woke early to the incessant buzzing of her mobile phone on her bedside table. Thinking it was the office, she reached for it and discovered something she hadn't expected.

The night before, while volunteering the graveyard shift at the Red Cross shelter on the University of New Brunswick Saint John campus, she'd met Ron Fairweather, manager of Domino's pizza on the city's east side.

He'd arrived with an offer: he'd provide pizza to anyone who wanted a pie, free of charge. An hour later, he returned with 20 pizzas. Impressed, Taylor took his photo, put a quick post up on her Facebook page, marked it "public" and shared it on the Saint John Newschaser Facebook Group.

(Brittany Merrifield photo)

PIZZA PIZZA

"Ron was just here from Dominos Pizza," she wrote on her newsfeed. "He has been going around to all the evacuee and volunteer sites and bringing free hot pizza for everyone. After Ron left we fed a family of seven and the mom cried and thus I cried as well. Also a family from Switzerland gave us bags of Swiss chocolate eggs for everyone. Some happy kids here tonight. People are good."

A lot of readers agreed with Taylor's sentiment. Her post was shared and reposted dozens of times and by the morning of May 4, people were messaging her from all over the city with offers of help, supplies and food.

"That's what I did for days. One time I got a call from a woman who said, 'My kids and I are in our car just leaving Moncton, where do you want us to go?'" said Taylor of the volume of calls, emails, private messages and posts she answered.

"I'd be so exhausted from sandbagging — which by the way is the worst job ever — and then I'd get another call. I think that feeling that brought people out, it's bottled now. If there's another situation and someone says, 'we need 300 people over here for this family,' no problem. People are going to show up."

(Above) Ron Fairweather, manager of Domino's Pizza in East Saint John delivers pizzas to the Red Cross Shelter and promptly becomes a social media sensation thanks to Chris Taylor's post.

(Left) A growing pile of sandbags to help residents of Grand Bay-Westfield.

(Right) In Grand Lake, water rose to the level of street signs.

(Below) Chris Taylor's social media posts brought people out to help with the volunteer sandbagging effort in Saint John.

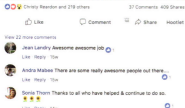

THE MIGHTY RIVER

For 20 days in spring 2018, the Saint John River reasserted its power over the land and people of central and southern New Brunswick. Water barrelled through the southern reach of the river at more than nine million litres (328 thousand cubic feet per second — four times its normal rate — damaging more than 12 thousand homes, cottages and buildings, washing out roads and bridges and requiring $39 million in federal disaster relief.

The 2018 Saint John River flood was historic not only for what it did, but also for what it represented. This was New Brunswick's eighth climate-related natural disaster in six years, all caused by fresh water — rain, snow and floods.

According to the New Brunswick Department of Environment and Local Government, climate change will lead to warmer winter temperatures, a rise in total precipitation falling in fewer but more intense events, more frequent winter thaws and larger fluctuations in river runoff.

Check, check, check and check.

"I believe there will be more events and we need to start preparing for what comes next," said Saint John Fire Chief Kevin Clifford. "Those of us in disaster relief have a term for that: build back better. Citizens are always going to want to be close to nature but maybe we could take a step back."

Historical Floods in New Brunswick
Source: New Brunswick Department of Environment and Local Government

A massive ice jam flooded these homes outside Fredericton during a 19th century flood.

1696
A late and very high freshet caused late planting and crop failures at Jemseg and the French settlers considered abandoning the settlement.

1701
After this flood, which caused losses to crops and cattle, the French settlers did abandon Jemseg for Port Royal on the other side of the Bay of Fundy in what is today Annapolis Royal.

1789
At Prince William, Kingsclear, Queenbury and French Village, ice damage during the spring freshet destroyed houses, barns and hay as well as killing stock animals belonging to 20 families. Ice was piled 40 feet high in Maugerville and the force of the ice destroyed elms and maples.

1831 or 1832
Cause: While there is confusion from newspaper reports as to whether this flood occurred in 1831 or 1832, it is clear the flood was significant. An ice jam downstream of Fredericton caused significant flooding, so much so that in just a two-hour period it reached levels higher than 1887.

Affect: Both the upper and lower parts of Fredericton were underwater. At Queen Street, water was two to four feet deep and water flowed upwards as far as Regent Street. The Keswick Islands were flooded and some homes floated away.

1885
Cause: Summer freshets on the Upper Saint John River caused the water to rise 16 feet at Van Buren, washing away the new Grand Falls bridge.

Affect: The Saint-Basile flats were flooded and throughout the system, lumber booms were broken, wood lost, houses and mills carried away and bridges collapsed.

1887
Cause: Ice jams, heavy snow accumulation melting, heavy rains on April 29 and 30 and a high spring tide in the Bay of Fundy all conspired to create a major flood that caused an estimated $500,000 damage.

Affect: The flood began April 26 as the ice began running and a serious jam occurred upstream of Woodstock. When the jam released, water rose five feet (1.5 metres). By May 2, a second jam had formed at Douglas, backing water up 40 kilometres and submerging the nearby islands. That same day, the ice ran out at Grand Falls and eyewitness reports stated the water had never been as high.

In Woodstock, water peaked on May 6 or 7, before receding May 10. Flood waters washed out the rail line and rail communications with the west was suspended from May 2 to May 13.

Cost: Maugerville-Sheffield was the hardest hit, with water halfway up people's homes. No division was visible between Grand Lake and the Saint John River.

1923
Cause: Snowmelt, combined with heavy rain, warm temperatures from April 28 to 30 and a high spring tide, caused a historic flood. At Van Buren, above Grand Falls, water flow was 134,000 cubic feet per second.

Affect: At the mouth of the Nashwaak River, water levels rose 3.4 metres between the morning of April 29 and the afternoon of April 30, then began falling on May 1. The Kennebecasis River, which was experiencing its second flood of the spring, recorded high levels and in Hampton boats were needed to get from the village to the train station, the first time that was needed since 1887.

Cost: Caused around $10 million damage and impacted most of New Brunswick. Two men drowned — the first when his boat overturned in the Magaguadavic River and the second while trying to save his livestock at Musquash. The provincial public works department estimated damages to roads and bridges to be at $450,000, half of which occurred in the Saint John River basin.

Officers Square in Fredericton during the 1887 flood.

Downtown Fredericton looks like a lake during the 1887 flood.

Two men canoe around Officers Square in Fredericton, circa 1887.

People used rafts and canoes to get around Fredericton after streets were flooded during the 1887 flood.

1936

Cause: High temperatures and two days of rain caused an unusually early spring break-up, resulting in ice jams and flooding that caused extensive damage.

Affect: At Saint Leonard, water levels rose to within four feet of the International highway bridge. Peak flow in Pokiok (present-day Saint John) was 231,000 cubic feet per second. The water level in the Oromocto River was the highest in memory, according to the oldest residents in the community. At Gagetown, buildings on Main Street were partially submerged and the CNR bridge was destroyed.

Barns filled with hay and machinery were swept away at Hampstead and Wickham in Queens County. In Fredericton, the area from York to Westmorland streets and back to Argyle Street and the southern portion of Victoria Street were flooded, forcing people to their second floors of homes and businesses. The Minto subdivision of the CPR was under water for about 10 kilometres.

Cost: An estimated $2 million in the Fredericton area alone. About 28 provincial bridges were destroyed or damaged as well as the CNR bridge in Fredericton.

1973

Cause: An above average snowfall coupled with an extra-tropical storm on April 27 caused rivers to rise rapidly to historic levels, peaking on April 29 and 30. The Saint John River below Mactaquac Dam reached a daily flow of 393,000 cubic feet per second on April 30.

Affect: During an ice jam, the water level on the St. John River rose to 8.9 metres, which is nearly 7.6 metres above summer level. The flood produced the highest water ever recorded in Fredericton.

Cost: The total economic cost of the flood was estimated at $11.9 million. Damage in the Fredericton area and to the agricultural land downstream accounted for about 60 per cent of the total economic cost of the flood. One death was reported.

2008

Cause: Record-breaking snowfall, about 50 per cent above normal, a late spring thaw, heavy rains and warm weather caused water levels to rise rapidly along the Saint John River and its tributaries.

Affect: The communities of Maugerville, Jemseg, Clair and Barkers Point saw the worst of the flood. About 50 streets were completely or partially closed in Fredericton. Across the province, 1,000 people were evacuated from their homes and at least 2,000 people were affected by the flood.

Cost: Flood damage exceeded $23 million and about 631 properties with affected; some homes beyond repair. A number of homes in the Fredericton-Oromocto area were condemned.

2018

Cause: Driven by strong currents and even stronger winds, the flood came faster than anyone could ever remember. On May 4, near Maugerville, the Saint John River reached 1973 levels — 2.17 metres (7.11 feet) above sea level.

Affect: Over a 20-day period, the Saint John River reasserted its power over the land and people of central and southern New Brunswick. Water barrelled through the southern reach of the river at more than nine million litres (328 thousand cubic feet per second — four times its normal rate — damaging more than 12 thousand homes, cottages and buildings, washing out roads and bridges. The total number of buildings damaged was 12,947.

Cost: The total cost is estimated at $80 million. The New Brunswick government would cover about $15 million, with the remainder, $65 million, covered by the federal government.

(Michael Hawkins photo)

2

RIVER PEOPLE

(Opposite) Mary-Faith and Todd Mazerolle survey the damage to the living room of their home in Newcastle Corner, on the shores of Grand Lake. Mary-Faith's family, the Baileys, have lived in this area since the original land grants.

"I'm going to warn you, I'm a crier."

Mary-Faith Mazerolle is standing on her front lawn, staring at what used to be her home. From the outside it looks fine, a ranch-style bungalow with large picture windows that look out over Grand Lake, the largest freshwater wetland in New Brunswick.

On this summer afternoon, the lake lies peaceful and calm across its more than five thousand hectares. But look a bit closer and you'll notice some things aren't quite right at the Mazerolle's property.

The front deck is missing, making the front door, which faces the lake, unusable. Instead, the deck lies several metres away around the corner past a small stand of trees on the other side of the driveway. The only way into the house is through the back door, which means stepping up onto a couple of wobbly cinder blocks.

There used to be back stairs underneath the carport but those stairs now sit a bit askew, halfway down the long driveway, still largely intact, complete with metal bannister. Both the deck and stairs were torn from the house by the massive waves and winds that pounded Grand Lake during the 2018 flood, leaving both where they fell when the water finally receded.

Inside, the house is a shell. The flooring is gone, as is the insulation. The bottom half of all the walls have been torn out, revealing the wood frame. Waterlogged furniture has been disposed of, leaving behind small personal items that survived — a fruit bowl, Nancy Drew novels and a plaque that reads "Faith, Family, Friends."

"Right now, I'm still pissed off with Grand Lake," says Mazerolle, her back to the water. This is a new emotion for her.

The property, located on a point that juts into Grand Lake at Newcastle Centre near the northernmost part of the lake, has been in her family for generations. "The land has been in my dad's family [the Baileys] since the original land grants," she says. "Each of his siblings got a piece of property."

This is where Mazerolle learned to swim and to fish, and it's where all her strongest memories reside. "We'd get up in the morning, put our bathing suits on and take them off at night."

ABOVE FLOOD LEVEL

Like many lake residents, Mazerolle's parents lived through the 1973 flood and so when they built the current home in 1989 they built well above that flood level, with a four-foot crawlspace rather than a full basement.

Each year during the spring freshet they'd watch the water levels rise on Grand Lake, but it never threatened the house. It's why Mazerolle and her husband Todd were confident they could safely go on a Caribbean cruise — their first vacation in 20 years — at the end of April, leaving instructions with their teenaged son Owen to monitor the freshet and call his uncle, an electrician, if anything happened.

In the first few days of the flood, as the Mazerolles frantically tried to stay connected with their family back home, the water rose higher than it ever had before and soon there was six inches of water in the house. Then the wind picked up.

"The wind and the waves busted through the front door," says Mazerolle. "My brother went out and bought $500 worth of plywood to nail up over the windows but by the time he got back the wind and water had already broken through."

The plywood went back to the store, unused.

"Just this winter we did $40,000 in renovations. The contractors were finishing it up as we went away. We didn't get to use our new bathroom before we had to throw it all away," says Mazerolle with a deep sigh, as she stands amidst the detritus where the new floor had been, pointing at a pristine oval mirror, the manufacturer's label still in place.

IF DAD WAS HERE

She closes her eyes as the emotion of what has happened rolls across her face. "Dad passed away three years ago. He and Mom designed and built this place themselves. I keep thinking if he was here he'd know what to do."

Mazerolle wipes tears from her eyes and looks out at the lake with a rueful smile. "He loved this place. Dad always used to say you can get anywhere in the world by boat from Grand Lake, New Brunswick."

That's true.

(Above) In Grand Lake, buildings were ripped from the ground and left to float, lopsided in the flood waters.

(Right) The Saint John River basin extends from its headwaters in Maine, through Quebec and into New Brunswick. The 2018 flood impacted the area from Fredericton to the river's mouth in Saint John.

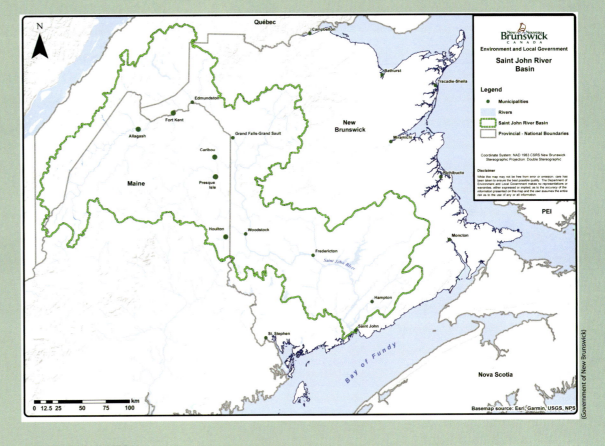

820 METRES
The highest point above sea level in New Brunswick is Mount Carleton. It is located near Nictau Lake, the headwater for the Tobique River.

SAINT JOHN RIVER

Saint John River is arguably the most historically and culturally significant river in Canada, having been a primary transportation route for the movement of animals, people and goods dating back to the last ice age.

The river, which lies within the Appalachian region of North America, is the second largest watershed east of the Mississippi River, surpassed only by the St. Lawrence River, according to the Canadian Rivers Institute, an aquatic science research centre at the University of New Brunswick. In 2011, it published what is still considered the definitive scientific analysis of the river basin, "The Saint John River: A State of the Environment Report."

The river basin, which includes tributaries, marshes and wetlands that drain into the main stem, covers 55 thousand square kilometres, 51 per cent of which lies in New Brunswick, 36 per cent in Maine and 13 percent in Quebec.

(Left) A view of Saint John River near Public Landing, pre-flood.

THE TRIBUTARIES

It has nine significant tributaries: the Allagash River, in Maine; the Aroostook River and Mexuxnekeag River, both of which run through Maine and New Brunswick; the Madawaska River, which is shared by Quebec and New Brunswick; and the Green, Tobique, Nashwaak, Oromocto and Kennebecasis rivers, all of which are in New Brunswick.

The lower reaches of the river, which lie below Fredericton, include five major lacustrine (related or associated with lakes) bodies of water: Grand Lake, Washademoak Lake, Belleisle Bay, Long Reach and Kennebecasis Bay.

The river itself is 700 kilometres long, beginning its journey from its headwaters in northern Maine and making its way through three distinct physical geographic regions, beginning with the Chaleur Uplands, known for its rolling hills and valleys.

Around Woodstock, the river enters the Miramichi branch of the New Brunswick Highlands, known for its steep slopes and fast-moving streams. At Mactaquac the river passes into the Maritimes Plain, the flattest part of the river basin, home to bogs and the basin's two largest lakes — Grand Lake and Washademoak.

(Above) Mary-Faith and Todd Mazerolle stand on their deck, which had been attached on the opposite side of the house and was carried through the stand of trees to the right in the photo and deposited just beyond their driveway.

(Above) Mike Roy uses a personal watercraft to pull a dock loaded with a hot tub and lawnmower as floodwaters surround his home on Grand Lake.

(Darren Calabrese Canadian Press photo)

481 METRES
The amount the Saint John River drops from its headwaters to its estuary.

As it leaves Washademoak Lake at Hamstead, the river enters the craggy landscape of the Caledonia, or Bay of Fundy, Highlands where it turns and dips its way down to its mouth, which empties into Saint John Harbour via the narrow channel of rapids known as Reversing Falls.

Twice every day the Bay of Fundy fills and empties more than 160 billion tonnes of salt water. All that water combined with the unique shape of the bay creates a rocking effect, known as a seiche. It takes about 13 hours for the water to travel to and from the mouth of the bay near Grand Manan Island to its head in the Minas Basin. At the same time, the Atlantic Ocean's natural tidal cycle of 12 hours and 25 minutes reinforces the rocking motion, creating the distinctive high tides.

REVERSING FALLS

In Saint John, this natural phenomenon is on full display at the Reversing Falls gorge, where the powerful Bay of Fundy tides connect with the mighty Saint John River. Every six hours, as the tide is rising, it sits higher than the river and is able to reverse the river's flow, creating the famous effect.

As the tide goes out, it drops below the river's level, which resumes its normal course and is allowed to empty into the Bay. At the midpoint of this aquatic tussle is a 20-minute period known as slack tide, when the bay and the river are at equal strength. This is the only time in the tide cycle that boats may pass safely through the rapids.

The tidal effect is so powerful it can be felt as far as the Mactaquac Dam, 140 kilometres upriver.

"It's the most famous entry into the ocean anywhere — and it's right here. It's ours," says Molly Demma, executive director of the Saint John River Society, a non-profit that promotes the wise use of the river's natural and cultural resources.

This is a river with many stories to tell. In 2016 archeologists unearthed an ancient encampment near Fredericton with artifacts dating back more than 12 thousand years to a time before the river itself. The camp was along the shores of a glacial lake that stretched from Fredericton to Belleisle Bay and was likely 10 times the size of Grand Lake.

Another site, located at the foot of Bentley Street in Saint John, a stone's throw from Reversing Falls, contains artefacts that date back 10 thousand years, further evidence of continuous human habitation. In fact, most of New Brunswick's thousand known archaeological sites date from this time period.

"Think about that," says Demma. "The pyramids are five thousand years old. We have 12 thousand years of stories."

(Left) The Renforth Wharf in Rothesay on the Kennebecasis River.

THE BIRCH-BARK CANOE

The river's famed birch-bark canoe was developed to traverse the river about three thousand years ago and extended Indigenous trading routes, which archaeological evidence suggests included a significant network that extended deep into the Ohio River valley.

Europeans arrived in 1604 when Pierre Dugua, the Sieur de Mons, and Samuel de Champlain sailed into the mouth of the river to establish France's land claim in the new world. Champlain named the river "Saint-Jean" to mark the day of their arrival, June 24, the French feast day of St. John the Baptist.

Acadians were the first Europeans to settle in the river valley, in the early 1600s. They lived here continuously in small settlements until the mid-1700s when the Expulsion of the Acadians saw the remaining Acadians either flee north or die at the hands of British soldiers.

As colonial traders, explorers, missionaries, fishermen, soldiers and settlers began to explore and establish permanent residences and fortifications along the river, the rhythm of life for the Wolastoqiyik was violently and tragically disrupted.

Following the Expulsion, British forces pushed the Wolastoqiyik away from the mouth of the river and to places farther north, while settlers moved in. Maugerville was the first successful English-speaking settlement on the river, founded with the arrival of New England planters from Massachusetts in 1763-64.

(Above) Canoeing is a popular and common activity in the river basin, which came in handy as a means of transportation during the 2018 flood.

213 METRES
The highest waterfall on the main river is in Grand Sault/Grand Falls. It has a vertical drop of 23 metres.

LOYALISTS ARRIVE

United Empire Loyalists began arriving en masse in 1784, creating the City of Saint John at the mouth of the river the following year. Others journeyed up the river to the former French settlement of Pointe Saint Anne, which they renamed Fredericton and declared the provincial capital of the newly created British colony of New Brunswick. This area was chosen because it lay astride the river and was as far as ocean-going ships could travel at the time.

Fredericton became home to a large garrison because soldiers could travel quickly down and up the river, all the way to the St. Lawrence River, connecting the new Maritime settlements with Quebec and Montreal. To the south, people could travel to Halifax, the newly created United States, Great Britain and the rest of the world beyond via the Bay of Fundy and the Atlantic Ocean.

The river's ability to connect to the world led to the creation of a substantial shipbuilding industry. At its height in the mid-1800s, the Port of Saint John was the largest wooden shipbuilding centre in Canada and the fourth largest in the British Empire. As the St. John River Society describes it, "At the height of the industry, over 8,000 white pines per year were floated down the Saint John River to Saint John for use as British navy ship's masts."

The river was the primary source of transportation throughout the 1700s and 1800s, first with wood boats, schooners and canoes, then with steamboats, would not be supplanted until the arrival of railways in the late 1800s, followed later by modern highways in the post-war boom.

(Right) A man walks down Campbell Drive in Rothesay that was flooded by the Kennebecasis River, one of nine tributaries of Wolastoq/Saint John River basin.

(Michael Hawkins photo)

(Left) A worker with the Atlantic Coastal Action Program (ACAP) in Saint John conducts field research in Wolastoq/Saint John River basin.

(Opposite) The beauty of the flooded Wolatoq/Saint John River at night near Maugerville.

THE MOST DISRUPTED

According to the Canadian Rivers Institute, Saint John River is one of Canada's most disrupted river systems. It has been subject to industrial forestry in its headwaters in Maine through northern New Brunswick and along its tributaries for more than a century. It is home to Canada's third largest potato crop, centred around Florenceville, and it has a high concentration of poultry and hog farms.

It is also home to a number of hydroelectric dams and reservoirs, most notably NB Power's trio of dams along the river's main stem — Beechwood, Grand Falls and Mactaquac — that have altered aquatic life.

The river basin supports a population of more than five hundred thousand people, the vast majority of them in New Brunswick and living in rural and urban communities the entire length of the river, from Edmundston to Saint John.

"The grandness and scope of this river can overwhelm us," says Demma. "It's just so huge and so vast and I think sometimes in telling the story of the river we scale it down to a regional level, to a human level, so we can make sense of it. However, when people have an opportunity to learn about the totality of the river, it fills them with a huge sense of pride.

"It's like the flood waters flow through all of us. When you boil it all down, we are river people."

This is how it has always been for the Wolastoqiyik, Indigenous people who have lived alongside Wolastoq watershed for thousands of years. They are the original river people.

(Below) Rothesay resident Jon McEachern's view as he and one of his dogs paddle down a street in their flooded neighbourhood.

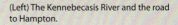
(Left) The Kennebecasis River and the road to Hampton.

(Steve Dionne photo)

BEAUTIFUL AND BOUNTIFUL RIVER

"Our language is very verb-y," explains Ron Tremblay, Grand Chief of Wolastoq Grand Council. "It describes what a thing does, everything always has a purpose." Breaking the river's name down, Tremblay explains that "Wol" means good or great, "ast" means to bring together and "oq" expresses location. Put it all together and Wolastoq, pronounced Wuh-luh-stuhk, is meant to encompasses the central role the river plays in the lives of its people — the Wolastoqiyik, the people of the beautiful and bountiful river.

"We don't separate the spiritual, from the governance, from the science in our language," says Tremblay. "That river was our main source of life. For fish, for food, for transportation, for cleaning and for cooking. Along its banks we grew and harvested our medicines and our food, such as fiddleheads and berries."

Like many in New Brunswick, Tremblay learned about the river through his family's stories and the stories told by neighbours and Elders. For instance, his grandfather, who grew up along the Negot/Tobique River (Negot means where one river flows underneath another river) remembers picking medicines and fishing along its banks, before the hydroelectric dams were built in the 1950s and 1960s, obstructing the flow of fish and flooding the banks.

FREEZE THAW

Northern New Brunswick gets a lot of snow and it varies from year to year. So, too, does that snow-water equivalent, which is the amount of water in the snow. This, more than snow depth, is what the New Brunswick Hydrology Centre monitors for the spring freshet.

By the beginning of March 2018, the province had 112 per cent the normal amount of snow than in previous years. By mid-March, the amount had dropped a bit, to 92 per cent, all within the normal range for New Brunswick.

By mid-April, however the Hydrology Centre recorded snow levels at 134 per cent, evidence that very little snow had melted. This snow pack, heavy with water, proved to be one of the big issues with the 2018 flood.

(Above) The Royal Kennebecasis Yacht Club clubhouse, located at the confluence of the Saint John and Kennebecasis River, was surrounded by water on the eve of its 150th anniversary celebrations.

(Below) The Kennebecasis River threatens backyards and homes in Rothesay.

A TRADITION

Unlike European culture, which favours a written narrative, Wolastoqiyik culture, like many Indigenous cultures, adheres to an oral tradition of recording and sharing of its history, which means the stories Tremblay and others tell reach deep back in time to the end of the last ice age and the origins of the Wolastoq River.

That was the era of Kiwhosuwicik, or Muskrat people who were dying of thirst because they could not access any water. Aglebe'm, a river monster was sitting at a point on the land blocking all the water from flowing.

The people sent a message to Keluwoskap (Glooscap) asking for his help and so he went to see Aglebe'm and asked him to release the water. He refused and so Keluwoskap cut a great tree, which fell on Aglebe'm, killing him. The tree became the river, its branches the branches, or tributaries, of Wolastoq and its leaves the ponds and streams.

TRYING TO CATCH UP

"This is how we became Wolastoqiyik," says Tremblay. "Our Indigenous knowledge is our science. It is centred around our relationship and connectedness to the land and to the water — and western science is just beginning to catch up."

Indeed, it is. In 2009 Cecelia Brooks was invited to tell the river's creation story at a forum hosted by the Canadian Rivers Institute. When she was done, biologist Allen Curry approached her. Curry studies the ecology of fishes and a few years earlier he had set out to answer this question: how did fish and animals populate the river basin?

In 2007, he published the results of his research, concluding that fish had recolonized what is now eastern Canada via the upper St. Lawrence River valley into the upper Saint John River. However, the fish were stopped above Grand Falls because a debris field, caused by retreating ice, prevented further movement. As it melted and cleared, the river was able to flow, enabling fish and animals to move south into the newly formed watershed.

Brooks smiles as she tells this story.

"I used to say science and Indigenous knowledge should go together, but now I think Indigenous knowledge (IK) should go first because if we had that as a starting point, we'd have the context and know where to start to look," says Brooks.

"When western science first dated the time of that glacier at Grand Falls, it was timed at about eight thousand years ago and I said, 'no you're wrong, it's older, that's what our stories tell us.' Well, lo and behold, archaeology has found settlements dating back 12 thousand years right on the river."

"Science and Indigenous knowledge are saying the same thing."

3

A RIVER ON THE RISE

(Opposite) Fredericton's Sainte-Anne Point Drive and the parking lot behind City Hall.

They call themselves the Pine Boxers. As in, "The only way I'm leaving here is in a pine box." These are the people who have lived for years, many their whole lives, along Route 105 as it runs along the river in Maugerville, beyond Bluebird Corner, past the Big Potato, around the Burton Bridge and on towards Sheffield.

They know every inch of the place, having grown up on stories about Maugerville and Sheffield from parents, grandparents and assorted relatives. Some can even trace their ancestry back to the original English-language settlers, the New England Planters. A bit of the autonomous and independent spirit of those 17th century Protestant Congregationalists remains as well.

In Maugerville and Sheffield they pride themselves on taking care of their own, which means each spring a community-wide flood watch takes place. Beginning in mid-March, neighbours start chatting with each other, comparing notes, checking local indicators, such as "the flood tree," and sharing information with each other, particularly on the Maugerville Flood Watch Facebook Group.

In early April, chatter was sparse. There was the occasion photo of the river taken from a back deck or driveway with a comment or two about eyeballing the levels to see if it was lower or higher than the same day in previous years. Someone passed along information about the snowmelt in Aroostook County, Maine, home to one of the river's nine tributaries, while others posted questions about water levels and about the Mactaquac Dam.

Then April 26 arrived and with it, the spring freshet; but still no one panicked. Local MLA Pam Lynch cautioned that the area was expected to hit flood stage within the next 24 hours, while the Oromocto Fire Department reminded residents its members were going door-to-door that evening. "Couple of people are saying it's going to be worse than 2008," wrote Kyla Robinson. "Is that what's to be expected?"

"Keep your knickers on and don't believe the hype," wrote Markus Harvey. "Nobody but the good God almighty knows what's going to happen. Take it day by day and we'll keep you informed."

(Left) Fredericton's north side.

THE SPRING FRESHET

Freshets mark the arrival of spring on river systems throughout the northern half of North America. The cause is always the same: melting snow and ice caused by warming temperatures enter the river system, raising water levels.

Generally speaking, spring floods in New Brunswick fall into two categories: floods caused by ice jams, which tend to occur earlier in the spring, around late March, and water floods, which arrive in late April or early May. For instance, the 2012 ice jam that devastated Perth-Andover was caused by ice jams in the river, whereas the 2008 flood was caused by rising water.

"We didn't have an ice jam problem this year; April was a slow melt," said New Brunswick Emergency Measures Organization (NB EMO) manager Greg MacCallum, who was the official face and voice of the 2018 flood with his daily briefings. "What we had was a lot of snow, with a rapid melt that coincided with rain fall. That is what we got."

MORE SNOW THAN USUAL

According to New Brunswick's EMO, this year there was 40 per cent more snow than normal in the northern reaches of the river system and the snow itself was different too. The winter had brought fluctuations in temperature, causing the top layer of snow to melt, then freeze and then become covered with new snow, a cycle that repeated itself through the early months of the year.

That increased the water content of the snow by 40 to 50 per cent, which meant the snow pack was denser and wetter than normal.

(Below) Rothesay placed portapotties in flooded neighbourhoods after floodwaters from the Kennebecasis River flooded the town's sewage lagoons and pump stations.

FREDERICTON – 8.24 METRES
Peak flood level reached on Saturday April 28, 2018, 24 hours after the flood first hit Fredericton. This was the third highest level on record, surpassed by the 1973 flood (8.61 metres) and the 2008 flood (8.36 metres). Fredericton was the only community not to set a new water-level record in 2018. Flood level in Fredericton is 6.5 metres.

TAKING NOTICE

On April 23, NB EMO issued its first flood advisory through the River Watch program for the areas of Saint-Hilaire, Jemseg, Grand Lake, Sheffield-Lakefield Corner, Oak Point and Quispamasis-Saint John based on the Environment and Climate Change Canada forecast of above normal temperatures of 15-20 degrees C, nighttime lows of -1 C and rain in northern New Brunswick.

Two days later, on April 25, River Watch issued another advisory: much of the Saint John River would reach flood stage in the coming days, beginning with Fredericton on Friday, April 27, followed by Maugerville and Jemseg by 7 a.m., Saturday, April 28.

LOW-LYING AREAS

None of this came as a surprise to anyone living in low-lying areas of the river, nor were the projected river levels cause for concern. "You don't have finished basements down here," says Markus Harvey, explaining that residents of New Brunswick's floodplain measure all advisories against the historic high set by the 1973 flood.

"Everyone is set up for a normal freshet. We put things up high, we get our vehicle passes and we wait. I take the first week of May off every year. I either split wood or deal with the flood. For people down here a normal flood is kind of nice. They (the Oromocto Fire Department) close the roads for a couple of days, it's quiet and you just get to sit and watch the river."

Unbeknownst to the people living along the river, 2018 wasn't going to be a normal year.

(Right) Canoeing home along the swollen Kennebecasis River near Nauwigewauk.

(Far Right) Riding an old tractor down Route 105 in Maugerville.

(Left) An aerial view of homes in Fredericton flooded by the Saint John River.

FRIDAY APRIL 27: CAPITAL CITY FLOOD

Frederictonians woke up Friday morning to a flooded downtown. River levels had risen more than 2.5 metres in a single day, with levels vaulting over the flood stage of 6.5 metres above sea level to 7.85 metres.

The flood had arrived and it was ahead of schedule. The evening before, the City of Fredericton had issued a warning that flood waters were expected to rise to eight metres by Sunday April 29, but the river had other plans.

"This flood caught people off guard because it was fast and unlike past floods," said NB EMO's MacCallum. "Flooding of the Saint John River is progressive. You get it in the north first and then progressively you get the same impact through the whole system. The river is wide, narrow, deep, shallow, winding and straight. This is a problematic river system because the system fills up very quickly."

(Above) A neighbourhood greenspace in Fredericton is lost to the rising river.

(Right) The swollen river at Fredericton made Sainte-Anne Point Drive and the on-ramp for the Westmorland Street Bridge impassable.

THE RHYTHM OF LIFE

Still, most people in Fredericton weren't too worried. They were accustomed to the municipal parking lots behind city hall flooding with some water. This was part of the rhythm of life in the capital city and people were coming down to the river's edge to marvel at its power.

Meanwhile, the municipal government closed some downtown streets and staff at the Crown Plaza Fredericton-Lord Beaverbrook started sandbagging the parking lot, a low-lying area on the river's edge prone to flooding.

However, down in Maugerville and Sheffield, the pine boxers were getting nervous. "That Friday it came up six or eight feet in a day. That doesn't happen," said Harvey. "I was at work and my wife called to tell me it was getting bad and to come home."

He wasn't the only one getting frantic calls from family members. Farther up the road Cindi Hachey was caught off guard by the speed with which the water raced in on April 27. She and her husband live on the northernmost stretch of Upper Maugerville and that morning as she left to go for a speed walk at the Grant Harvey Centre on the other side of the river in Fredericton, she noticed there was a little bit of water on the far side of the road.

"When I came back two hours later it was over the road and near the Irving," she says. By lunch, she had called her husband, a civilian at CFB Gagetown, and told him to come home. "Then I made a grocery list and told him we're going out to get supplies because this is going from zero to crazy," she said. Hachey was worried the rising waters would cross the road in the low-lying areas on either side of them, isolating her in her home.

(Right) A woman captures photos of the flood in downtown Fredericton from a footbridge.

(Opposite) The off and on ramps for Fredericton's Westmorland Street Bridge are impassable.

MAUGERVILLE – 7.3 METRES
Reached its historic high flood level on Sunday May 6, 2018, 10 days after the flood began in Maugerville. It surpassed the 1973 flood (7.11 metres) and the 2008 flood (6.92 metres). Flood level in Maugerville is 6 metres

Hachey's concerns were justified. While her house never flooded, everything around her did. "We were pretty much trapped on our island for about three days."

SATURDAY APRIL 28 AND SUNDAY APRIL 29: MORE WATER THAN 2008

If anyone was in doubt about the size of the 2018 flood, they weren't by the end of that first weekend. Up and down the river system people were racing to protect their property from the floodwaters, while local first responders were assessing safety levels on roads near the river.

Route 105, which follows the river from Grand Sault/Grand Falls down to Youngs Cove on the eastern side of Grand Lake was flooding in low lying areas. Barricades went up in Florenceville-Bristol and in Hartland — home to New Brunswick's famed covered bridge.

Woodstock, which marks a change in the river's trajectory from the rolling hills of the Chaleur Uplands to the more rugged and faster moving path through the Miramichi Highlands, managed to avoid major flooding. The only concern in town was the local New Brunswick Community College parking lot after the Meduxnekeag River crested its banks.

Back in Fredericton the river continued to rise. By Sunday night, 40 roads were closed on both sides of the river and hundreds of parking spaces were underwater, all of which meant the Monday morning commute would be severely disrupted for hundreds of provincial civil servants.

The New Brunswick Legislative Assembly, with its distinctive copper dome, stands across Queen Street from the river's edge, enabling it to be seen from the city's north side and from the University of New Brunswick's campus at the top of College Hill.

This placed it directly in the path of floodwaters. So too was the nearby Sartain MacDonald Building, which housed the Department of Social Development, as well as Chancery Place, the new government office building attached to the Fredericton Convention Centre that housed the Premier's Office and Office of the Attorney General, as well as the departments of Aboriginal Affairs and Finance, and the Regional Development Corporation and Treasury Board.

(Clockwise from left) Scott's Nursery in Fredericton has flooded in the past but 2018 was particularly bad. The rising Saint John River almost reached the hanging baskets. However, there were almost moments of beauty, in the reflections of the greenhouse's bowed roof in the flood waters.

(Opposite) Officers Square in Fredericton is often flooded, dating back to the 1800s.

BUILDINGS CLOSED

As the water continued to creep into Fredericton's downtown, the Government of New Brunswick ordered its buildings in the flood zone closed, instructing employees to work from home. This included an area bordered by Queen Street to the north, University Avenue to the east, Dundonald/Beaverbrook Streets to the south and Smythe Street to the west and included the departments of Education and Early Childhood Development, Health, Justice, Post-Secondary Education, Training and Labour, and Transportation and Infrastructure.

Interestingly, four departments never threatened by floodwaters were the quartet most responsible for promoting and protecting New Brunswick's physical landscape. The departments of Agriculture, Aquaculture and Fisheries, and Energy and Resource Development stayed high and dry in the Hugh John Flemming Forestry Centre at the top of College Hill, while the departments of Environment and Local Government, and Tourism, Heritage and Culture monitored the flood from Marysville Place, kilometres from the river on the city's North Side.

On Sunday night, Anglophone West School District announced it was closing Barker's Point Elementary School on the city's north side and cancelled busing for the Connaught Street School because of its location within the downtown flood zone. The district also cancelled all or portions of bus routes in Rusagonis, Maugerville, Hoyt, Central Blissville, Perth-Andover, Fredericton Junction and Tracey.

(Left) Floodwaters penetrate deep into Meenan's Cove Park, submerging the beach and barbecue pits.

(Above) As the water began to recede in Maugerville, the high-water mark is visible.

The justice system needed to continue to function, flood or no flood. It activated its disaster plan and relocated the New Brunswick Court of Appeal and Court of Queen's Bench to UNB Faculty of Law main building, Ludlow Hall, and Fredericton's provincial courts moved downriver to the Burton Courthouse.

While downtown business owners debated whether to open on Monday, and civil servants prepared to work from home, across the river on the north side, city residents living south of the Princess Margaret Bridge were watching with horror as the water streamed up their streets and into their homes.

HOMES EVACUATED

The Fredericton Fire Department worked quickly to evacuate families from homes on Mcminniman Court and Burpee, Jarvis and Hossack Streets, with the aid of a floating motorized vehicle to rescue those whose houses were already surrounded by water a metre deep. Other residents got out kayaks, canoes and inflatable boats to maneuver around the neighbourhood or to check out what was happening nearby.

Tensions also began to rise as people struggling with the flood had to contend with visitors popping over to check out the flood and the City of Fredericton issued the first of what would be many reminders that anyone caught ignoring barricades would face a $172.50 fine.

Frederictonians weren't the only ones pulling out their kayaks. About 130 kilometres to the south, the residents of Darlings Island were confronting the reality that they were about to become isolated. The small island community is located on the Kennebecasis River, about 10 minutes from the Saint John suburb of Quispamsis to the west and the Town of Hampton to the east.

The island has a single access point; the Darlings Island Road bridge, which crosses a narrow channel to connect with Route 100 at Nauwigewauk. The road was closed Sunday afternoon, forcing people to park their cars on the mainland and wade knee deep across the bridge.

And still the river continued to rise.

4

WATERSHED DOWN

(Opposite) Flooding in the Spar Cove Road neighbourhood of Saint John on the city's north side.

Mike Carr wanted to know what was headed his way. A Saint John firefighter and manager of the city's Emergency Management Organization (Saint John EMO), Carr drove up to the Mactaquac Dam on Sunday to see how much water was racing through.

From there he travelled slowly back to Saint John, stopping in to talk with his colleagues at the Oromocto Fire Station and sticking to the river roads as much as possible, in order to get a feel for the flood. He, like other emergency responders, had been carefully monitoring the flood forecasts for the better part of a month and now he wanted to know what was happening on the ground.

"The practitioners said it's a lot more and it's coming a lot faster. Basically it's 24 hours ahead. What they said was coming on Tuesday was actually hitting you on Monday."

MONDAY APRIL 30: WELCOME TO SAINT JOHN

Saint John is the largest city on the river system and it is where the river connects with the sea. All the water rushing down from those nine tributaries and five lakes, from Maine, Quebec and the rest of New Brunswick, all of it barrelling towards Saint John and its famous Reversing Falls, the narrow passage that connects the river with the Bay of Fundy.

Flood stage in Saint John is 4.2 metres above sea level. On Sunday morning the Department of Environment's five-day forecast estimated the Saint John region, which includes the bedroom communities of Rothesay, Quispamsis and Hampton, could expect water levels of 4.4 metres on Monday. The city was forecasted to reach 1973 levels late Thursday evening or early Friday morning.

(Right) Surrounded in Upper Maugerville.

And that's not counting the tides. During the annual spring freshet, the Bay of Fundy tides act as a gate, halting the river's flow and forcing the river water back upstream where it naturally gathers in the estuary's larger bodies, such as Washamadoak and Grand Lakes.

In Saint John, where the tidal effect is at its strongest, planning for a flood means calculating two high tides each day, which will bring water levels higher than the provincial flood forecasts. Saint John EMO staff must calculate the effect of two powerful bodies of water at play in a relatively small area.

That's what Carr and his team were thinking about when they set out to inspect Saint John's flood-prone neighbourhoods Monday morning. "The biggest thing on day one for us was this: we are standing by South Bay watching the river and by the time we came back out, the road was underwater," he said. "That's how fast it arrived."

The areas most under threat were the residential neighbourhoods nestled in the low-lying coves and shoreline located where the Kennebecasis River flows into the Saint John River a few kilometres upriver from Reversing Falls. "Our biggest challenge during the flood wasn't homes being flooded," said Carr. "It was people being isolated."

Before the day was over, Saint John EMO closed the roads leading in and out of those neighbourhoods – Acamac, South Bay, Dominion Park and Milford – as well as the city's main riverfront artery, the Westfield Road.

> **OAK POINT – 5.95 METRES**
> Reached its historic high flood level on Monday May 7, 2018, eight days after the flood began in Oak Point. It surpassed the 1973 flood (5.74 metres) and the 2008 flood (5.36 metres). Flood level in Oak Point is 4.7 metres.

(Above) Some helping hands to move nervous cows to high ground.

(Right) Cows on a farm in the Maugerville/Sheffield area get ready to be moved as waters rise.

TUESDAY MAY 1 – TRAFFIC REROUTED

New Brunswickers woke up to the news of widespread closures, detours and warnings. Three river ferries in Evandale, Belleisle Bay and Summerville-Millidgeville had service suspended, forcing residents of the Kingston Peninsula to travel greater distances to reach the other side of the river.

About 800 homes in Saint John were in immediate danger of flooding but Canadian regulations do not give first responders the authority to issue mandatory evacuation orders. That left the SJ EMO with only one option: to issue a voluntary evacuation for about 1,900 people in the neighbourhoods of Dominion Park, Millidgeville, Randolph Bridge, the Westfield Road between South Bay and Morna, Gault Road Mellinger Crescent and Ragged Point Road as well as anyone living those living past the St. Francoise De Sales Church on Boar's Head Road.

An emergency shelter at Carleton Community Centre was set up to accommodate people being displaced, along with a Red Cross emergency shelter at the University New Brunswick Saint John campus, which was located on the border of the flood zone.

(Left) Sandbagging detail at The Pit in Grand Bay-Westfield, which lasted for a week and produced 18,000 sandbags.

In the bedroom communities along the Kennebecasis River, Rothesay set up a sandbagging station at the municipal arena, the QPlex recreation complex was partially converted into an emergency reception area and Quispamsis staff went door-to-door to about 230 homes to personally warn residents of the flood headed their way.

Upriver in Fredericton the water reached and then surpassed the 2008 flood mark of 8.36 metres, forcing the City to close its downtown offices and restrict traffic on the Princess Margaret Bridge, which traverses the river and is the main artery connecting to Minto to the east and Maugerville/Sheffield to the south.

"Residents who've experienced flooding in the past should expect to experience similar, and possibly worse, flooding in those locations over the next few days," cautioned MacCallum during his daily public briefing, as he explained a second surge was expected. "[The flood] continues to be dynamic and it's becoming increasingly complex. Levels are gradually but continually increasing."

A sandbag filling station in Burton attracted volunteers from both sides of the river.

QUISPAMSIS-SAINT JOHN – 5.73 METRES
Reached its historic high flood level on Monday May 7, 2018, eight days after the flood began in Jemseg. It surpassed the 1973 flood (5.31 metres) and the 2008 flood (5.2 metres). Flood level in Quispamsis-Saint John is 4.2 metres.

WEDNESDAY MAY 2 – REMEMBER '73

By now, many areas in the flood zone had reached or surpassed 2008 levels and the provincial EMO and local first responders were sounding a very loud alarm: the river would likely reach 1973 levels before the end of the week.

This flood was about to enter the record books, largely because of continued rainfall up north. Environment Canada issued a rainfall warning for Edmundston, Miramichi and Moncton, worrisome news for residents and first responders fighting back the river.

Corporations and community organizations were providing supplies and services to support emergency efforts. Cooke Aquaculture provided boats and sent more than 10 thousand sandbags to Grand Bay-Westfield. The Fredericton Capital Exhibit Centre had become a temporary home for about 50 sheep and horses with 70 cows expected.

The Town of Hampton closed parts of Main Street, while up at Hatfield Point on the Kingston Peninsula parts of Route 124 were underwater.

Amidst all this chaos, the New Brunswick government announced its aid package for residents: up to $160,000 for structural damage and up to $500,000 for small businesses and not-for-profit organizations for any damages not already covered by insurance policies.

(Above) Those who couldn't sandbag helped out by making dozens of sandwiches for the volunteer sandbagging crew in Grand Bay-Westfield

(Right) Cars drive through flood road in West Saint John.

(Left) Saint John Marina and other parts of Westfield Road were underwater. To the left is the train tracks used to transport residents out of the flood zone.

THURSDAY MAY 3 – TRANSCANADA HIGHWAY CLOSES

Residents of Chipman, a village of just over a thousand people located at the head of Grand Lake, found themselves isolated when both Route 10 and Route 123 were flooded over by the swollen Salmon River that reached a level of 6.6 metres, just over the 1973 mark of 6.45 m.

Emergency responders were available to ferry people to safety and trains were used to supply provisions. J.D. Irving, the community's major employer, reported that logs were floating in the yard of its pulp and paper mill.

J.D. Irving also provided a free train service to isolated Saint John-area residents via New Brunswick Southern Railway, which made four stops along the Westfield Road. Before the weekend was out, the train would deliver families, and at least one church minister who had a sermon to deliver on Sunday morning, to safety.

Canadian Coast Guard boats arrived from Halifax and the Canso Canal to assist with transporting residents to and from isolated areas, where the water was so high there were reports of otters and beavers swimming above front lawns. As the water continued to rise the TransCanada Highway was closed between Fredericton and Moncton at 7 p.m. because the river threated to flood at least one lane of the road. This effectively cut off cottage owners from their properties on the southeast side of Grand Lake, which meant all they could do was wait and depend on neighbours to send them photos, videos and text updates. It also forced normal traffic to take a significant detour through Saint John, doubling travel time between the two cities to two-and-a-half hours.

FRIDAY MAY 4 – ISOLATED

While water levels continued to hold in Fredericton, the river's other major urban centre was still battling rising waters.

City of Saint John crews were called in to build an emergency clay berm around the Milledgeville wastewater treatment plant to keep the water away. Without it, the river threatened to overrun the facility and cause untreated wastewater to run into the river. That was already happening because of the closure of 10 lift stations due to flooding.

For the fifth consecutive day SJ EMO recommended residents of the Westfield Road and adjacent areas evacuate; 190 people from 75 homes took that advice. "We came within 12 hours of 1,400 people being isolated on Westfield Road," said SJ EMO manager Mike Carr. "We put ATVs, a fire truck and a Works Department truck with medical and construction equipment in it . . . put it high and dry and staffed it."

Elsewhere in the province's six rescue boats from the Department of Fisheries and Oceans (DFO) and a Coast Guard patrol craft were deployed in Grand Lake while a Transport Canada Dash 8 aircraft conducted surveillance.

Meanwhile, help was offered from a number of faith-based organizations such as Samaritan's Purse Canada and Christian Aid Ministries Canada, both of which sent disaster-relief units to the flood zone, along with volunteers to clear out debris and support homeowners in tearing out insulation, wallboard and upholstery before mould set in.

(Above) Maugerville and Sheffield area farmers moved their livestock to the Fredericton Exhibition grounds, others boarded their cows with other farmers while others moved their cows to higher ground on their properties.

SATURDAY MAY 5 – WINDS FROM HELL

As the flood entered its second week, there were 30 emergency-responder vessels patrolling the waters between Saint John and Fredericton, on the lookout for people who needed help.

"Subject to availability and lack of higher-priority missions, support will be provided to people to keep them safe and secure in their homes," stated NB EMO's public alert. "This may include transportation to resupply groceries, gasoline, pre-scheduled, non-urgent appointments or other necessities."

Levels across the southern part of the river basin had surpassed 1973 levels — and this was having an impact on another river system. Water was rising on the Madawaska River in northern New Brunswick, caused by high water levels from the Saint John River and an increase in water outflow from the Temiscouata Dam in Quebec. Saint-Jacques residents in northwestern New Brunswick were warned to stay on alert for flooding and told sandbags were available.

And then came the wind.

Gusting up to 70 kilometres an hour in some parts of the province, it hampered rescue efforts and did significant damage to properties in the flood zone. It roared across Grand Lake, tearing through doors, breaking through windows and ripping cottages apart. In Saint John, the wind, in tandem with the rising tide, sent residents frantically back to sandbagging stations in a race to prevent the now sizeable waves from breaching the makeshift walls and flooding homes.

(Above) Wildlife such as deer and moose were forced to high ground during the flood in search of food supplies.

(Ken Redmond photo)

(Opposite) The front of a cottage was torn away by the violent winds and waves in the Maquapit Lake area, east of Sheffield-Lakeville Corner.

(Right) The Schryers needed a wall of sandbags and multiple sump pumps to hold back the Kennebecasis River from flooding their Quispamsis home.

After the wind died down, Delberta Flood made an unusual discovery as she walked along the shore near her home in Youngs Cove, on the south side of the lake. A fully-intact cottage, with the curtains still in the windows, had come to rest on the shore near her home. After posting a picture on the Grand Lake Facebook Group, Aaron Moore responded — the cottage was his and it had floated seven kilometres across the lake from his property in Princess Park.

"We saw some pretty weird things float by," Flood told Canadian Press, "but that's the weirdest."

SUNDAY MAY 6 – A SLOW RETREAT

The day began for most with some good news: the water was beginning to recede in Fredericton, although a weather-forecast prediction of 20 mm of rain in the northwest kept residents on edge. NB EMO said the water should crest in Saint John Tuesday around dinnertime, coinciding with the high tide, and then slowly recede into the next week.

(Michael Hawkins photo)

(Left) J.D. Irving's mill in Chapman was surrounded by flood waters.

(Below) No diving sign suggests the water level is normally a lot lower on this stretch of the Saint John River.

Maugerville residents woke to the startling news that Markus Harvey had been jostled from bed just before 5 a.m. by a trio of intruders breaking into his darkened, power-less home. "I jumped out of bed and they scurried," he wrote on the Maugerville Flood Watch Facebook group a few hours later.

He raced outside and was able to snap a photo of them as they made their way downriver.

"Three men wearing bandanas over their faces. From the look of the grainy pic I got of them, they're in a small canoe, no motor and paddles. RCMP are on their way. Farmers up and down the road are out in boats now looking for them. Last seen heading down river from my place towards Moxon's Country Pumpkin."

Before the day was out, the police would arrest and charge three local men.

(Above) Erika Betts kept track of rising waters by photographing the mailboxes near her home in Grand Lake.

MONDAY MAY 7 – NEW LIFE AMIDST THE CHAOS

With more than 100 roads and bridges still closed, Logan Pearson picked quite a day to make his entrance. His parents, Kathrin Wiede and James Pearson, had wanted a home birth but Logan and the river had other plans. Initially due on April 25, just ahead of the flood, Logan was 12 days late and by that time his parents and older sister Zoë had been flooded out of their Cambridge Narrows home.

The family had moved into the house in 2014 and had been told water had never reached the foundation. By May 1 there was three feet of water on their first floor and they were moving in with friends.

"I was exhausted," says Wiede of those last few stressful days before Logan's arrival. "We didn't get back into the house for three weeks." But May 7? "We are going to tell him it was a good day."

TUESDAY MAY 8 – PUBLIC HEALTH CONCERNS

Dr. Jennifer Russell, the province's chief medical officer of health, warned residents of water contamination from farmlands, compromised sewage systems and sewage backup from homes and businesses — not to mention all the debris from flooded and destroyed homes and cottages floating in the river, including hazardous waste such as barbeque propane tanks.

"If residents find sewage has backed up into their home, they should wear rubber boots and waterproof gloves if in contact with water and during cleanup," recommended NB EMO in its daily alert.

In Chipman, local EMO officials made arrangements for J.D. Irving to helicopter in Shoppers Drug Mart pharmacist Kelly Beam so residents could receive much needed prescriptions after being isolated for close to a week.

NB Power reported it had disconnected 952 customers because of flooding and advised residents they would have to have an electrician authorize their homes as safe before power would be reconnected.

About 85 roads remained shut or partially closed in the flood zone.

WEDNESDAY MAY 9 – SPRING RITUALS INTERRUPTED

High levels of contamination in the water prompted Public Health to warn people against eating fiddleheads, a popular spring delicacy, harvested from the flood zone. People were also advised to wait 30 to 90 days before planting vegetables, particularly green, leafy vegetables or root vegetables, in soil that had been flooded. It was a timetable that all but prevented weekend gardeners from sowing summer crops.

Saint John closed four public parks — Robertson Square, Tucker Park, Shamrock Park and Dominion Park — due to possible contamination.

(Left) Flood waters washed out low-lying areas such as in this South Bay neighbourhood in Saint John.

(Graeme Stewart-Robertson photo)

THURSDAY MAY 10 – MILITARY PROVIDE SUPPORT

As it turned its attention to clean-up and rebuilding, the Government of New Brunswick requested the Canadian Armed Forces perform a reconnaissance mission to determine how it could help.

About 60 members of the 4 Engineer Support Regiment at CFB Gagetown assisted with planning and co-ordination of relief efforts, assessing flood damage and advising on mitigation of key infrastructure.

"They're deploying to help their neighbours and the communities close to where they live," Rear-Admiral Craig Baines, Commander Joint Task Force Atlantic, told the Canadian Press. "Many of our members have been volunteering in recent days, like many community members have, at night and on weekends to help their neighbours."

FRIDAY MAY 11– THE PRIME MINISTER VISITS

Canadian Prime Minister Justin Trudeau toured the flood zone, praising community efforts.

"The clean-up is going to come in the coming weeks and months; it's going to be a real issue," reported the Telegraph-Journal. "The response of the folks who stepped up, the response of communities, of first responders has been extraordinary. There's a real strength of community."

The Government of New Brunswick announced it would conduct a full review of the flood and the response to it once initial cleanup was complete.

But the best news of the day was that the TransCanada Highway would partially reopen.

(Above) Cinder blocks, still attached to the floor of a cottage, floats on Grand Lake.

SATURDAY MAY 12 AND SUNDAY MAY 13 – WATCH OUT FOR MOULD

Residents began to return to flooded homes and cottages with a warning from EMO: beware of mould, contaminated household items and small debris, such as nails and broken boards that may have floated onto property.

MONDAY MAY 14 – SORTING FLOOD WASTE

Fredericton, Maugerville, Grand Lake, Oak Point and Quispamsis-Saint John began the week below flood stage for the first time.

Cleanup in rural areas and municipalities began in earnest, with pickup slated for May 21 in rural areas.

"Flood waste includes appliances (remove doors and covers for safety), furniture, carpeting, insulation, paper products, construction debris, etc.," stated the NB EMO daily alert. "Hazardous materials (i.e. petroleum and propane tanks, chemical containers, dead animal carcasses, etc.) will not be accepted."

TUESDAY MAY 15 – FUNDING FOR COTTAGE OWNERS

The Government of New Brunswick announced $6,100 for cottage owners to assist with cleanup. The federal Disaster Financial Assistance program did not cover the restoration of recreational properties.

Sheffield-Lakefield Corner dropped below flood levels just before dawn.

WEDNESDAY MAY 16 – FLOOD IS OVER

Jemseg was the last area along the river to return to pre-flood levels, which it did around lunchtime.

(Right) A view from the rooftops of Maugerville.

5

COTTAGE LIFE

(Opposite) An aerial view of a Grand Lake West cottage and its debris field.

Jen Nelson is not supposed to be here. She's supposed to be 115 kilometres away in Cumberland Bay, waking up to the smell of husband Jeff's pancakes on the griddle and the laughter of her kids as they get ready for another day at the lake. Today, though, she is sitting on the worn easy chair in the Rothesay coffee shop overlooking the parking lot of a strip mall on a foggy summer morning.

"It's gone," she says, staring down at her half-empty cup. "I am a fish out of water."

The Nelsons may live in this Saint John-area bedroom community, but their hearts are in Cumberland Bay. That's where their cottage was until the powerful winds of May 5 broke through the picture window, allowing the waves to crash in and carry off a lifetime of memories.

Both had spent their childhood summers on Grand Lake, or the Lake as it's known to locals. Jen Nelson's dad was in the military, which meant she moved around a lot. The family cottage at Youngs Cove was her favourite place, where she could hang out with her extended family. She was baptized at the Youngs Cove United Church and her grandparents, aunt, uncle and godparents are buried in its cemetery.

A PLACE OF PEACE

Eight years ago, the Nelsons had saved enough to purchase their own cottage in nearby Cumberland Bay.

"At our cottage we don't have Wi-Fi and the kids loved it. It was our place of peace," she says. "We were seven years without a deck and last year my husband worked hard to build it. Well the deck is still there, we just don't have anything to connect it to."

(Left) Despite being mounted high on wood supports, the water reached Mark Ellis's Grand Lake West cottage and completely destroyed it.

The couple — she's a massage therapist, he's a school principal — can't afford to rebuild and will likely sell the land with the hope of finding another property higher up. They, like many cottage owners, spent their summer sorting through insurance documents, trying to figure out if they could receive some compensation for the destruction caused by the wind and waves.

"The day before cleanup we were staying at my aunt's place just down the road and for the first time in my life the sound of the water was not comforting."

Grand Lake has been a popular cottage destination for over half a century because it enjoys some of the province's warmest temperatures. The area has two municipalities — Minto and Chipman — and a ribbon of rural communities on either side of the lake, which are home to permanent and seasonal residents. To the southeast are the communities of Cumberland Bay, Youngs Cove, Whites Cove and Robertson Point.

Along the northwestern bank in what is known as Grand Lake West are the communities of Douglas Harbour, Princess Park, Sunnyside Beach and Newcastle Creek. Grand Lake is the largest lake in New Brunswick and acts as a heat sink for the Saint John River basin. During the spring freshet as the Bay of Fundy tides restrict the river's drainage at Reversing Falls, excess water can remain in Grand Lake for days, as it did in 2018.

(Below) Shingles and a front porch will need to be replaced on this Whites Cove cottage.

(Above) This was once a cottage.

(Right) Shirley and Gordon MacDonald built this cottage from reclaimed barnboards in 1967. It was destroyed by the 2018 flood.

HAPPY MOTHER'S DAY

For cottagers, Mother's Day weekend normally represents the start of their favourite season. It's time to open the cottage, reconnect with neighbours and get ready for another summer at the lake. Instead, many families spent the next couple of weeks surveying the damage and trying to figure out what would come next.

"We are so devastated," says Nancy Carter, as she sits with her mom, Shirley MacDonald, in a Fredericton Tim's, flipping through photos on her smartphone. "We used to watch these things on TV and think, 'those poor people,' and now we're those poor people who had everything and now have nothing."

Shirley and her late husband, Gordon MacDonald, built the family cottage at Whites Cove from old, reclaimed barn board in 1967 after buying the small parcel of land for $300. They lived in Riverside-Albert and Shirley, a nurse, wanted a summer place to take their three kids. It was bare bones in those early years, with two sets of bunk beds and an outhouse for the family of five.

"It was our last link to Dad and now it's gone," says Carter, of the cottage where she and her siblings grew up, surrounded by a close-knit multigenerational community that was facing the possibility that life on the lake would never be the same. "One of our neighbours who didn't flood says her biggest fear is people won't come back."

(Above) Initially the Carters had planned to open their cottage the week the winds came.

(Left) The water laps at the door of Nancy Carter's cottage in Youngs Cove.

CAN'T REBUILD

With an estimated price tag of $40,000, Carter says she and her husband can't afford to rebuild but they know they don't want to leave the lake. Of the 20 cottages in their neighbourhood, 11 were destroyed.

Initially, Carter thought the cottage would be okay. Her neighbour had been keeping an eye on the properties and had texted her on Friday, April 27, to tell her water at her cottage was at a normal level for the spring flood and she would be good to open the cottage for the season the following weekend.

The next morning, water had reached the cottage and by Sunday her husband decided to drive out to the cottage and raise the appliances off the ground. "We figured a foot off the ground was safe," says Carter. "We're about 200 feet from the water."

By Wednesday, May 2, the Carters were being advised to pack hip waders. They moved mattresses to the top bunks as about a foot-and-a-half of water flowed in. They went home to Miramichi and waited for news. "On Saturday our neighbour called. 'Nancy, it's bad,' he said. 'Your cottage and mine are floating.'"

Carter pauses and looks out the window as she gathers her thoughts.

"We are still numb. Our front wall is gone," she says. "I came home with a Sobeys bag of stuff. That's all we could save."

The neighbour's cottage now sits behind Carter's while parts of other cottages lie strewn through the back woods. There's a sauna and shower in perfect condition standing upright. Clothes lie everywhere, as do pieces of walls and roofs.

"Whatever demons of hell were in that cottage I'll never know," says Carter, shaking her head at the memory of seeing it for the first time. "Well that's not true, is it? We know. It was the waves."

Some neighbours have already started to rebuild, lifting their cottages five or six feet in the hopes of avoiding the next big flood. Shirley laughs ruefully at the thought of so many familiar places up on stilts. "If we do rebuild like that I'll have to be Tarzan to get in the front door."

In the Petrie family, they aren't cleaning up one cottage; they're cleaning up three. Three months after the flood Jamie, his brother Richard and their mom Connie are still coming to terms with the immensity of what occurred.

(Right) After the water receded, the damage was done to the Carter cottage in Youngs Cove.

(Above) A message from happier days stuck in a tree where it landed once the water subsided.

(Left) Caution tape, a floating gas tank and 50 years of memories of the Petrie family's cottage in Robertson Point.

> **JEMSEG – 6.74 METRES**
> Reached its historic high flood level on Sunday May 6, 2018, nine days after the flood began in Jemseg. It surpassed the 1973 flood (6.36 metres) and the 2008 flood (6.11 metres). Flood level in Jemseg is 4.3 metres.

MULTIGENERATIONAL STORY

Like most families on the lake, theirs is a multigenerational story. Connie had grown up by the lake and in 1968 she and her husband Gordon built their own cottage next to her parents on Robertson Point.

"It was fantastic to grow up around huge family gatherings," remembers Jamie Petrie. "I lived at Grand Lake my entire youth. I didn't play sports in the summer; I just wanted to be at the cottage. I'd go down at the end of June and I'd come back in time for the Fred Ex."

His brother eventually inherited their grandparents' cottage and in 2009 Petrie and his wife Giselle decided to purchase their own cottage at nearby Whites Cove.

"It's a hell of a lot of work to run two places, to worry about two places," he says. "I can't tell you how many times in winter we'd sit in Fredericton during a big storm wondering how our place is. But there's a reason we put up with all that heartbreak and cost… There is something spiritual or emotional about sitting there at the lake."

When they aren't at the cottage, the Petries live in Fredericton and as they watched the river stream down city streets on April 27, they started to worry about their trio of cottages. While Jamie flew out to Toronto for business, Giselle drove up to Youngs Cove to move items and small appliances to higher ground. The previous year they had put a small addition on the cottage at the back and she thought things would be safe back there.

On May 1 Jamie flew back into New Brunswick on the 7:30 p.m. flight and the couple whipped down to the cottage to move the washer and dryer, beds and refrigerator.

"We were doing it all with flashlights, it was nuts." Two days later the TransCanada Highway closed, cutting off the Petries from their cottage. For the next seven days the Petries could only wait, depending on updates from permanent residents John and Loreen Hunter.

(Below) The Petrie Cottage in Whites Cove.

(Above) The waves roll by Connie Petrie's cottage in Robertson Point, destroying it.

(Right) Some cottages could not withstand the 70 km/hour wind gusts that rocketed through the Grand Lake region.

HEROES

"They're heroes. They opened their home up to a lot of families," says Petrie. Once the water started to subside, John called Petrie. "'I think you should buy a lottery ticket,' he said and my heart sank because I thought he meant I was going to need it. But then he said, 'you are incredibly lucky.' And we were."

Water had busted through one of two doors, flooding the kitchen and a second room. However, the frame withstood the onslaught, which Petrie credits to the new addition acting as an anchor to hold the cottage in place.

His mother was not as fortunate.

"Mom celebrated 50 years in that cottage this year and it was destroyed," says Petrie. "But she had such an amazing response. Incredible really. 'I had 50 wonderful years and I'm grateful for that.' That's what she says. She was more concerned about my brother and me. That's such a typical mom response."

The cottage Petrie and his brother grew up in was torn down, along with other cottages. On the weekend after the flood, as they drove around Youngs Cove and Robertson Point, the roads were clogged with dump trucks, tractors and pickup trucks hauling away the remnants of these seasonal communities.

"Robertson Point was shocking, it was like a picture you see of a tornado. I was so overcome with emotion," he says. "Everyone I saw was either in tears or in like a catatonic state. I felt so bad for all these neighbours I know and love."

DEVASTATED

The sadness and devastation prompted Petrie to do something he's never done before: write a letter to the editor of his local newspaper, The Daily Gleaner. "What motivates me to write this morning is the decision to discount the expense and devastating loss that these owners are experiencing," he wrote.

"Some cottage owners have invested more in these recreational properties than in their primary residences. Many live in these properties for almost half the year. Not only have they contributed to the New Brunswick economy year after year through their ownership and maintenance of these properties, they also pay a second set of property taxes on these properties for which many do not receive full services. In many cases, their loss due to the flood is no less devastating than any other loss experienced in New Brunswick this year."

In New Brunswick, cottage properties are classified as non-owner-occupied residences by the provincial tax system. This means owners of these properties pay both provincial and local or municipal property taxes, whereas owners of owner-occupied residences (a primary home) are not required to pay provincial taxes.

That tax bill can make it financially difficult to renovate or rebuild. "There are still a lot of people hurting," says Petrie shortly after the New Brunswick Day long weekend. "A lot of people haven't rebuilt because they can't afford it. That's sad because they put a lot of blood, sweat and tears into their cottage."

This is the question Adam Harris' extended family faces as they consider the future of their multigenerational cottage just down the road from the Petries at Robertson Point. The cottage was built in 1957 by Harris' maternal grandparents, Ralph and Annie Gill, and today is shared by Harris' mom Susan and her sister and best friend, Heather Bird.

"It never had a drop in 61 years and we had to tear it down," says Harris, his voice quiet as he sits in his Fredericton office. Robertson Point is where he has celebrated major family milestones, where his memories of his maternal grandparents are strongest and where his mom and aunt have spent some of their best days.

(Above) The refrigerator from sisters Susan Harris' and Heather Bird's Robertson Point cottage sit half a kilometre away, the little French chef magnet still in place.

(Left) Cinder blocks, still attached to the floor of a cottage, floats on Grand Lake.

GRAND LAKE – 6.82 METRES
Reached its historic high flood level on Sunday May 6, 2018, eight days after the flood began in Grand Lake. It surpassed the 1973 flood (6.45 metres) and the 2008 flood (6.24 metres). Flood level in Grand Lake is 5 metres.

PERFECT STORM

"It was a perfect storm, the highest tide of the year, the freshet and the wind. It was the wind storm that broke its back," says Harris. "When your roof line is cratered, it's a good indication it's more than just water damage."

The Harrises and Birds, like most cottage owners, arrived after the flood to find their belongings gone, including heavier items such as their refrigerator, which they found on its side half a kilometre away. "The fridge magnet was still on it — a little French chef holding a fork. It's so random."

Harris says the family will rebuild because life on the lake is too important for them to walk away. While they don't know how or when they will rebuild, Harris says his mom and aunt want to ensure the building is able to withstand what is likely to be an increase in intense weather.

"There's a myriad of questions coming out of it. What techniques should we use? Pilings or foundation? What flood level do you build to? How do you rebuild? Can you rebuild? How do you adapt? Do you just accept things are going to flood? It's a lot to think about," he says. "This was a remarkable event, a never before seen calamity. It reminds you that we are just on this rock spinning around. Our earth is pretty dynamic."

(Right) Jen Nelson's beloved view from her family cottage during happier days. The cottage was destroyed in the flood.

(Jen Nelson)

(Michael Hawkins photo)

6

ANGER AND LOSS

(Opposite) Nancy MacQuade Webb waves to passing boaters from her dock at the Gagetown Marina, which sustained $500,000 in damages and was closed for three months.

It is a perfect summer's afternoon in mid-July. The sun is shining and there's a slight breeze as Nancy MacQuade Webb, owner of the Gagetown Marina, stands on the dock waving to boaters as they motor down the river. Normally they'd probably stop in to refuel and grab a bite to eat at the Old Boot Pub, which MacQuade Webb also owns, but not today.

The Gagetown Marina is closed, as it has been since the 2018 flood came to town. The Village of Gagetown sits in a crook of the river, where the river turns southward and exits the lakes on its journey past the Kingston Peninsula and on towards Saint John.

The area was a fertile fishing and hunting ground for the Wolastoqiyik. The original European settlers were Acadians, who named the area Grimross. Following the violent Expulsion of Acadians from the area, the land was granted to Sir Thomas Gage by the British for his service during the Seven Years War and renamed Gagetown.

Father of Confederation Sir Samuel Leonard Tilley was born here and it was long a stop for steamboats and riverboats, during the 19th and 20th centuries. Today, the village is known as an arts-and-culture hub, home to the annual FollyFest music festival and artists' studios.

THE HUB

It's also a hub for boaters, situated in the perfect spot for those travelling between Fredericton and Saint John, which has allowed MacQuade Webb to build a nice little business serving the people of Gagetown and their summertime visitors.

SHEFFIELD-LAKEVILLE CORNER – 7.01 METRES
Reached its historic high flood level on Sunday May 6, 2018, eight days after the flood began in Sheffield-Lakeville Corner. It surpassed the 2008 flood (6.45 metres). Numbers are not available for the 1973 flood. Flood level in Sheffield-Lakeville Corner is 4.8 metres.

"Irving says I have five times the fuel sales of all other marinas on the river," says MacQuade Webb, as she walks into the pub and sits down at a table near the door. It's almost lunchtime but the place is quiet, as is the main street, which on a Friday in July should be busy with tourists and day shoppers. But that activity is dependent on the marina and pub being open.

MacQuade Webb, like many New Brunswickers affected by the flood, applied for assistance from the provincial government's Disaster Financial Assistance program, which provided assistance for eligible damage and losses that threaten the health and safety of people, small businesses and municipalities.

Private homes were eligible for a maximum of $160,000 while not-for-profits and small businesses could apply for up to $500,000. After receiving an application, the government sent out inspections teams to assess health, environment, electrical and structural damage. For severely damaged homes, the government offered owners a buyout at market value and appended the property's zoning so the land could never be developed again.

Amid the stress and sadness of the flood's aftermath, few people had much praise for the program's slow speed of delivery and lack of timely information.

"All they've told me is I'm approved for assistance," says MacQuade Webb. As a business, she can apply for up to $500,000, which is what MacQuade Webb says she'll need to get her two businesses started again.

Gagetown, like Maugerville and Sheffield farther up the river, is low-lying, which means some flooding always occurs during the freshet. MacQuade Webb knew that when she and her late husband Gerry Webb bought the marina in 2004. They bought the pub in front the following year. Both had run successful businesses — she in public relations and he in financial services.

(Left) Cars float in the water in Maugerville.

(Below) The river remained high for days, reflecting life in the flood zone.

(Above) An aerial view of Maugerville.

(Right) Flooded out in Maugerville.

FLOOD PARTY

They were there for the 2008 flood when water levels reached 6.11 metres at nearby Jemseg. One of their docks became unmoored and they held an impromptu flood party on it with musician friends, beer and a healthy sense of humour.

An artist friend memorialized that day with a painting on the wall of the marina. That year the marina was closed for 10 days. In 2018 it was three months. "This is a seasonal business. I usually open the Thursday before the May long weekend and I close the Saturday after Thanksgiving," says MacQuade Webb.

Living on the Saint John River and running the Gagetown marina and local pub was a dream come true for the couple, two New Brunswickers who had met mid-life in Calgary, married and decided to return home. Gerry died in November 2017 and as his wife prepared for her first season without him, the flood came crashing through.

"The power of the river is mind boggling. If you didn't see it, you wouldn't believe it," MacQuade Webb says, as she flips through a small pile of unpaid bills. It will cost her $100,000 to replace the fuel system, including lines and tanks, the latter of which now sit upended near the road, at the opposite end of the marina yard.

(Left) Dramatic view of the Saint John River in Maugerville.

(Above) Giselle and Jamie Petrie's cottage property was littered with debris from other cottages from all around Grand Lake that washed ashore in Whites Cove.

The waves and wind yanked out all the electrical pedestals, which were available at each berth; replacing the electrical system will be another $200,000. She figures she had seven feet (2.13 metres) of water in the basement of the marina, which ruined the private showers and bathrooms.

"The fuel tank costs $20,000 and I'm sure the guy is going to want his $20,000 when he delivers it," she says with a rueful laugh, adding another contractor has stopped work until she has the money to pay him. "I have begged and borrowed from everyone. This is my only source of income. The government gave me a small advance and I gave everyone a little bit so they can work."

A COMMUNITY'S RESILIENCY

By early August, things were looking a bit brighter in Gagetown. MacQuade Webb was able to open the marina just in time to welcome boaters for the New Brunswick Day August long weekend, which this year was capped off with a special celebration. The village hosted the High and Dry Festival to celebrate the community's resiliency in the face of the river's wrath.

There's one more thing to celebrate too: 2018 marks the 100th anniversary of the building that houses the pub and marina.

4,957
Number of homes damaged by 2018 flood.

2,228
Number of cottages damaged by 2018 flood.

"I do love it here. It's a beautiful little village," says MacQuade Webb. "But you know, even in the short time I've lived here I've noticed the summer season has shifted almost a month. Summer doesn't really get going until July and it's beautiful into October."

Paul and Tina Arthurs have noticed changes too. They love to hunt and snowmobile throughout the Saint John River basin and they have watched the northern reaches change over the years. Paul blames clearcutting, which has reduced the forested areas in northern Maine and New Brunswick, while down around his home in Maugerville he wonders what effect the highway bridges and the berm built for the TransCanada Highway near Jemseg may be having on the river's volume and flow.

(Right) Paul Arthurs is lifting his house five feet to avoid damage from future floods.

1,250
Number of non-residential buildings damaged.

4,512
Number of vacant buildings damaged.

12,947
Total number of buildings damaged.

(Markus Harvey photo)

(Left) The access road to Darlings Island was flooded out, forcing residents to canoe, kayak or boat through the trees, past the outdoor rink and through to the island and their homes.

UNLIKE OTHER FLOODS

The Arthurs know one thing for certain: the 2018 flood didn't behave like other floods. They are accustomed to flooding. They live on Route 105, about halfway between the Burton Bridge and McGowan's Corner. Each year they follow the same routine. When the water reaches Perth-Andover they start planning.

On day one, as it approaches Fredericton, they clear out the yard. On day two, as it enters Fredericton, they clean out their garage and, depending of the flood forecast, on day three they put everything on the first floor up high.

"Nashwaak Bridge and Durham Bridge are always the first to go under," says Tina. "But all of a sudden we're hearing that Fredericton is going to hit flood stage. Well that didn't make sense."

The couple got the yard and garage ready and thought they'd be fine. On April 28th Paul went to bed at 1 a.m. with water seven inches from the deck. Two hours later he woke to the sound of his phone. "Our son Tyler called to ask if water was in the house. 'What?' I thought. 'Why would it be in the house?'"

He raced downstairs to discover Tyler was correct. Water was filtering into their first floor, so Paul quickly grabbed some paint cans to lift all the appliances off the ground.

Tina says this was different too. "It never rises at night." She pauses and adds, "My father warned us. He's a CBC person and he's also always listening to the farmers. He warned us of a major flood."

Not that it would have made much of a difference for the Arthurs' home. The water and wind that came barrelling through their yard in late April and early May wasn't about to let much stand in its way. It took out their garage, the pool, the deck and all the doors on the house.

(Below) Jacking up the Arthurs' house.

UNLIVEABLE

With their house unliveable, the Arthurs moved into their hunting trailer, which they set up at the end of their driveway. It had a bed, a galley kitchen, a small table and some chairs. Insulation poked out from one wall. "It's rough," says Tina. "It's not meant to be lived in."

The force of the water carved a six-foot hole that took 35 truckloads to fill. "There was so much current here during the flood, you couldn't stand up," says Paul. "Water takes off out of here at rocket speed. Then it gets caught in the lakes and it goes in and can't get out." As the crow flies, the Arthurs' home is a short distance from the Portobello Creek Nature Wildlife Area, which marks the entrance to French and Indian Lakes that feed into Maquapit Lake and then Grand Lake.

"I bought this house when I was 23 years old. Now I'm 53 years old and I don't want to do this again," he says with a grimace. It's why they've decided to lift the house six feet. "If my house floods again, the water is going up Smythe Street."

(Right) Paul Arthurs stands in what used to be his swimming pool, ripped apart by the river's fast current.

(Markus Harvey photo)

The Arthurs are under no illusions about the cost and frustration associated with such an endeavour. They put in a claim through the provincial government for $191,000 in damages and in late July received a cheque for $67,000. After the 2008 flood, they put in a claim for $67,000 and received $19,000.

"It's costing us $20,000 to $30,000 to lift the house," said Tina. "And it's all on our dollar."

By mid-August many of their neighbours were still waiting for payments. Some, like the Arthurs, weren't able to live in their homes due to the severity of damage.

(Left) Eldon Hunter, owner of Hunter's One Stop in Douglas Harbour, which was a central meeting place for information about the flood.

(Right) Maugerville damage.

(Far Right) The water came in so fast people didn't have time to move their vehicles.

THE ONE-STOP

Eldon Hunter has listened as friends and neighbours have wrestled with difficult decisions regarding their permanent residences and cottages in Douglas Harbour. Hunter's One-Stop lives up to its name in this little community on the northwestern edge of Grand Lake. Hunter never lost power during the flood, so this is where people came to buy supplies, exchange news and seek answers to some of their questions.

"I had one woman ask me if she could still use the English cucumbers in her Lady Ashburn pickles or should she peel them," Hunter smiles and leans forward over the counter for emphasis. "I told her she was fine."

He's had people ask about claims forms; he prints them off the store computer. Others wanted to know when the Twin Bridges would re-open. He called up to Fredericton to find out.

From his place behind the cash, near the door, Hunter hears and sees just about everything happening in Douglas Harbour. He knows some people who have taken the government buyout rather than attempt to rebuild. He also knows some local contractors who will be busy for months renovating properties.

CONFUSION

"Look, people care and the complaints are legit," he says. "No one knows what's going on. No one up there says to the district engineer, 'Go talk to people and tell them what you are doing.'"

Janet Kidd's house on Darlings Island survived the flood unscathed; it's getting home that's the problem. The island has a single access road and in 2018 it flooded, forcing residents to rely on water transportation to get to and from the mainland.

Kidd is a music instructor, which means she often works well into the evening, which is what happened one night during the flood. "It was raining a bit and it was super dark. I hadn't paddled in the dark for many decades and never alone," she remembers of the one-kilometre trip that took about 30 minutes to complete. "It was a conquer-your-fears moment. You have to know how to paddle through the trees. At the end of it, there is no one there to help. You just go haul the canoe on shore and go find your car and sometimes that was another half-kilometre walk."

(Below) Stairs that once were attached to a cottage lie in the middle of the woods with other debris in the Grand Lake region.

| 73

(Left) A heartbreaking loss for a family on Grand Lake.

ROAD REPAIRS A MUST

Residents have long petitioned successive governments to fix the access road by raising it above the flood level. This would require the government to acquire land along the current road, and while the government says it began those negotiations in January 2018, it doesn't have a firm date for when or if the project will begin.

"The message I'm hearing is there is no hope in hell of getting the road fixed before the next flood. We're very angry," says Kidd. "I saw people wading in chest waders. If we are all in this together and everyone is treated the same way no one would be angry. But that's not what we see."

Local MLA Pam Lynch heard that complaint a lot as she travelled through her riding of Fredericton-Grand Lake in the heart of the flood zone. A self-described country girl, Lynch was answering constituents' questions while also dealing with her own flooding issues. Both her home and her cottage were threatened by the rising waters.

"We lost a set of stairs, never did find them," she says with a laugh.

While she had praise for the leadership of NB EMO, she was frustrated with the lack of on-the-ground information regarding road closures and detours. She says constituents were calling and texting her with many questions and she had a difficult time finding them answers.

"I had to dig for information," she says, adding the work crews did a good job collecting garbage and keeping people safe during the flood. "It's important to communicate with people and keep an open dialogue."

(Below) Debris lines the stern of Markus Harvey's boat in Maugerville.

(Above) Electrical wires are still attached to a cottage floating in Grand Lake.

(Right) Grand Lake underwater.

ROUTE 690

For instance, during the flood the Twin Bridges, which are on Route 690, the main artery leading into Douglas Harbour and the Grand Lakes area, were closed, isolating people on either side. "No one would give me any information. It just made my job harder," she says. "I just wanted to know when it was going to open again."

To stay connected, Lynch used social media and in particular Facebook, where she was a regular contributor to five groups, each for a different part of her riding.

"If I hadn't had social media to provide updates I don't know how I would have known what was going on," she says. "I'd get home after a day of touring the riding and there would be 20 messages from people. I answered every one of them before I went to bed."

Social media was a lifeline to information and support for many people, not least of all Markus Harvey. He kept up a daily blog on the Maugerville Flood Watch Facebook group, describing life in the flood plain with wit and good humour — and the occasional jab at the provincial government.

SURFER DUDE

For instance, on May 5, he whipped out his board shorts and decided to hit the waves: "Good Afternoon Surf Team," he wrote.

"You could imagine my absolute glee when I looked out this morning to see the water had risen with a lovely swell and the potential for cooking up some juicy barrels to ride! I put on my boardies, grabbed my surfboard, ran downstairs … and then realized … I live in Maugerville; it's an epic flood, and the only barrels I'd be riding would be floating oil barrels while dodging driftwood kicked up by the high winds. Bummer."

A bit of humour for what had otherwise been difficult days. On Monday, April 30 Harvey's wife and three sons moved in with an assortment of friends in Fredericton, while he remained behind to keep an eye on their house and the houses of their neighbours up and down Route 105.

"I was the only person down here who didn't have power for eight days," he said. "In a flood, power is key. I made breakfast on the barbeque and used a lawn chair with a hole in it for a toilet."

He and the few other people who remained got into a rhythm, checking on each other and the homes around them by boat and powering up the gas generator to charge their mobile phones and connect with family and friends online.

"When I had no power that was the most surreal time. The house is dirty, no one is talking, there's no power so dishes aren't getting washed," he said. "There were dark days for sure."

THINGS MAY CHANGE

Harvey estimates there are about 700 houses in Maugerville and only a handful of people living between Bluebird Corner and the Burton Bridge who didn't grow up in the rural community. This flood, he fears, may change that.

"Government wants to have the perception of helping but they make it difficult and mired in paperwork. I know some people here haven't even registered [for disaster relief] because they don't want to be bothered. We've got our doctor and a couple of engineers and other than that it's seniors, farmers and regular folk.

"They don't have $40,000 in the bank account to raise the house or fix it on the hope that the government will pay them," he says. "Instead, people are poking away to get their homes livable, hopefully in time for winter. There's a whole line of trailers down here."

He pauses, looks out his kitchen window to the road he grew up on. "The landscape down here and around Sheffield is going to dramatically change. I think families aren't going to move back. The flood is moving people out quite nicely."

(Above) Maugerville's Markus Harvey used to live in Australia and had fun with his old surfboard in one of his lighter Facebook posts.

(Michael Hawkins photo)

7

FORECASTING THE FLOOD

(Opposite) Grand Lake permanent resident Erika Betts stands in her destroyed kitchen. She wants to know why there was no warning of the storm.

Erika Betts stares at her car, parked in the driveway of the Grand Lake home she shares with her boyfriend Mike Derrah. "Do you think it's salvageable?"

Unlikely. The car was completely submerged beneath the waters of the Saint John River at the height of the flood.

"We are basically at a standstill," says Betts, as she picks her way through her destroyed kitchen, careful to avoid stepping on the electrical cords, power tools and other construction items that litter the now unfinished floor. "On April 28, there wasn't a drop of water on this property; by Monday [April 30] we had to get the canoe out."

The young couple, like so many other permanent residents of the lake, have spent months waiting for disaster relief funding from the province. They were told they were approved, but for how much they don't know; nor do they know when the cheque will arrive. That's upsetting because the pair didn't just lose their home; they lost their businesses too. Both are tattoo artists and operated from the garage in the back of their property. Today Derrah is upstairs, in a makeshift studio, working on a new piece for a client.

"Our garage door was torn off. We had the neighbour's deck in our backyard," says Betts. "We are basically at a standstill."

Up and down the river, just about everyone has an opinion about what caused the flood. What everyone can agree on is the water came in very fast. People want to know why, and they want to know why no one in the NB EMO was able to warn them in time.

(Left) Simon Barton, left, and Chelsea Burley wear makeshift waders of garbage bags and packing tape as they cross a flooded road in Saint John.

NO WARNING

NB EMO manager Greg MacCallum understands residents' frustration with the lack of warning that significant flooding was on its way.

"That's the hardest piece to predict and I understand the public's critique of this," he said. "What happened was the rate of the melt exceeded expectations. The model underestimated it."

The challenge in 2018 was the amount of water in the snow. Normally, as snow melts, it absorbs part of melt back into itself. That's why in early spring, snow can appear thick, wet and almost soupy. This year, however, the weather had fluctuated up north causing the snow to melt, freeze, get absorbed back in the snow and get covered by new snow.

Then it rained, far more than forecasters had predicted. On the first day of the flood, forecasters had predicted 20 mm of rain. Instead, northern New Brunswick received 40-50 mm. The rain continued for a full week. That rain, coupled with dense, wet snow, caused the river to rise up in a historic flood.

New Brunswick's flood forecasting is produced by the Hydrology Centre within the Department of Environment and Local Government. This is how it works: first thing in the morning the team receives a weather briefing from the Atlantic Storm Prediction Centre in Dartmouth, Nova Scotia, which gives them the daily high and low temperatures, barometric pressure, wind speeds and direction, and chance of precipitation.

Next, the centre's data technologist collects all the information from the water-level gauges located all along the river in Maine, Quebec and New Brunswick. This information is then given to the forecast engineer, who combines the two sources of data to create the hydrological model, which calculates how much water is coming down the river.

This information is then shared with NB Power, which uses it to calculate how much water will need to pass through the dam.

$80 MILLION
Early estimates for total cost of 2018 flood. The New Brunswick government would cover about $15 million, with the remainder, $65 million, covered by the federal government.

$11,877,007
Total cost of damaged caused by the 1973 flood.

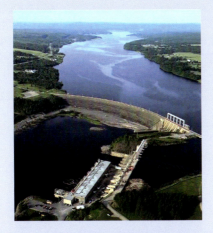

(Above) An aerial view of the Mactaquac Dam.

THE MACTAQUAC DAM

Mactaquac Dam, like the Grand Falls and Beechwood dams upriver, is a run-of-river dam. That means the holding pond created by the dam doesn't actually store much water. That's because of the Saint John River's geography, which is too small and narrow to allow for a large storage area. Instead, the water that flows into the Mactaquac head pond flows quickly through the dam's turbines, creating hydroelectricity. Any water not used for power generation must bypass the dam through its spill gates.

During normal operations, water passes through the dam at 2.27 million litres (eighty thousand cubic feet) per second. However, the 2018 spring flood produced far more water. On April 27, the first day of the flood in Fredericton, water was passing through Mactaquac at 8.41 million litres (297 thousand cubic feet) per second, over three times its normal rate. The next day — when the flood reached Maugerville — the water was at 9.26 million litres (327,000 cubic feet) per second. It did not return to normal levels until May 13.

To enable the water to flow through the dam and its spill gates, the river must approach Mactaquac at a downward angle, just as it used to before the dam was built. In order to achieve this slope, operators lower the head pond, which is why, according to NB Power and NB EMO, the head pond was so low during the flood.

THE HYDRAULIC FORECAST

Once NB Power has calculated its discharge levels for the day, the number is sent back to the Hydrology Centre to make a third and final calculation: the hydraulic forecast, which calculates the height of the water.

This requires three numbers: the hydrological forecast (water flow), NB Power's water-discharge estimate, and the height and timing of the Bay of Fundy tides. This final number allows forecasters to determine how much water will be able to pass through Reversing Falls and how much will be held back, left to linger in the lower reaches of the river basin.

It is the hydraulic forecast that is delivered to NB EMO and then published on River Watch.

There is one fact on which residents, experts, scientists and first responders can all agree: the five-day forecast is really a best guess, thanks to New Brunswick's fast-changing weather patterns. The flood forecast, just like a regular weather forecast, increases in accuracy the closer it gets to the actual day.

New Brunswick was the first province in Atlantic Canada to introduce flood forecasting and flood mapping, which it did following the last historic flood, in 1973, basing its new system on the one developed for Manitoba's Red River basin.

Brian Barnes was one of the people tasked with creating it and remembers all too well the challenges of predicting Maritime weather patterns.

"The problem with flood forecasting in the East is weather. It happens very fast in a small area and the biggest problem is forecasting where the rain is going to fall," he said, looking out at the Saint John River from his living room in Fredericton. "By comparison the Red River is very big."

(Above) Some residents still managed to find humour in the situation. Duncan Hazen Bridges snapped a pic of this sign in his grandfather's cottage in Maugerville.

(Left) A resident paddles his canoe at Darlings Island as the Kennebecasis River flooded the only road into the community.

FLOOD FORECASTING

The basis of flood forecasting is much the same now as it was then. To determine the level and speed of a flood, forecasters need to understand weather, rainfall, snowpack up north, daytime and nighttime high and low temperatures. Combined, these factors give an indication of how fast or slow the snow will melt in the upper reaches of the river system, in Maine, Quebec and northern New Brunswick.

A second factor is the topography along the riverbanks. Snow melts at different rates depending on its location. It melts first in developed areas, where streets, parking lots, driveways and turf will speed the melt, sends it quickly into storm sewers and out into the river.

Next, snow will melt in open fields such as farms, meadows and cut woodlots. Lastly, snow melts in forests. Trees slow winter melts in two ways: first, the tree cover shields the snow from the sun's warming rays, and second, the tree trunks, roots and branches slow the water's passage.

Barnes says a lot has changed in New Brunswick over the past four decades. "Human geography was different then. The province was more rural," he says, adding that over the years economic considerations have oftentimes taken precedence over ecological realities.

"We came out with flood-risk mapping so the public could understand, but local politicians, real-estate associations, municipalities and planning committees didn't want to limit development."

Matt Alexander understands too well the push and pull between land development and environmental protection. An environmental engineer by profession, Alexander is also the deputy mayor of Rothesay, a bedroom community that experienced flooding this year along the ribbon of residential development that runs along the banks the Kennebecasis River.

"One of the first projects brought to us after I joined council was a property owner who wanted to build close to the water. I voted against it but it ended up getting approved," says Alexander. "That person did flood this year."

(Above) Debris floats in Maquapit Lake area, east of Sheffield-Lakeville Corner in front of a flooded-out cottage.

(Right) Fredericton downtown saw Officers Square, Sainte-Anne Point Drive and city parking lots flooded out.

813
Number of Disaster Financial Assistance applications as of August 10, 2018.

220
Number of Disaster Financial Assistance applications paid as of August 10, 2018.

298
Advanced payment request paid out of a total of 302 as of August 10, 2018.

(Left) Kayaking around flooded neighbourhoods was common during the flood.

CHANGING LANDSCAPE

Across the river on Long Island, Alexander says he sees the landscape changing as more people use the land, cutting down trees to improve their view of the river. It's further evidence, he says, of New Brunswick's longstanding practise of allowing low-density development, known as ribbon development, sometimes through granting exceptions to planning bylaws, and sometimes by simply not prosecuting offenders.

"Over the years, we've really seen the Department of Environment [be] whittle[d] away. There really isn't anyone out there to enforce the rules."

Alexander says stronger enforcement of existing regulations under New Brunswick's Watercourse and Wetlands Alterations regulation (WAWA) is a good place to start. In the wake of the 2018 flood, the provincial government announced plans to introduce new requirements for people and developers applying to build near rivers, streams and brooks, to prove that the project will withstand future flood damage.

The existing WAWA regulations, however, only apply to buildings within 30 metres of a watercourse or wetland — and the 2018 flood destroyed buildings set much farther back from the shoreline.

Shawn Dalton understands the difficulty in trying to limit river-facing development along the Saint John River. She is a Fredericton-based social ecologist and one of the authors of the Canadian Rivers Institute report on the Saint John River. She recognizes that the desire to live and work along the river runs deep in New Brunswickers.

(Below) Rothesay resident Jon MacEachern walks his dog near the end of Campbell Road.

(Above) Leaves and debris indicate the high-water mark in Rothesay.

(Right) The view from the swollen river of Erika Betts and Mike Derrah's home, garage and shed in Grand Lake.

STORM SURGES AND FLOODS

"We have a big problem on our hands when it comes to storm surges and floods. We're on water and we will not back off it," she says. "People expect the river not to move but rivers move. Rivers wander around their flood plains and flood plains are big. If you build in a flood plain you are going to get slammed."

Dalton says that as more trees are removed from the shoreline — whether through industrial-forestry operations, agriculture, residential development or because of individual property owners with a simple desire for a view of the river — people can expect greater degradation of the shoreline, including erosion and flooding.

As people search for answers as to why the 2018 flood happened, Dalton suggests now is a good time to consider how and where New Brunswick permits development on the river.

"We see more and more people moving out into the country and building with an urban aesthetic. I'd like to know if there were different impacts of the flood on people because of shoreline management," she says. "We created this. It's a climate event — and this is going to happen more."

8

EMERGENCY CREWS AT WORK

(Opposite) Oromocto Fire Department trucks working in the flood zone.

When the old timers started coming out, that's when Chief Jody Price knew this was a flood like no other. The head of the Oromocto Fire Department trusts the instincts of the seniors who live up and down the Saint John River.

Every spring, before the freshet arrives, he likes to drive over the Burton Bridge for a coffee and a chat with some of them to gauge their opinion about what kind of flood season they think it will be. Those conversations serve two purposes: they give Chief Price insight into community opinions and help him strengthen the connections between the local fire service and the residents it serves.

"This year they were saying it was a warm spring so if it comes, it's going to come fast," he says. "This year acted just like 2005."

ANSWERING THE CALL

During a flood, the Oromocto Fire Department serves an area of just over 2,500 square kilometres, making it the largest Regional Emergency Operations Centre (REOC) in the provincial EMO system. It serves the Town of Oromocto as well as the rural areas of Maugerville, Sheffield, Burton, Geary, Rusagonis, Wasssis, Lincoln and Grand Lake.

Normally, it is a composite fire department with a force of 53 people, 23 paid and 30 volunteers. During the flood that number rose to 150 people as NB EMO reassigned provincial public safety and natural resources officers to the local flood detail.

With such a wide area to cover, the region was divided into four divisions: Water Division for boats, Alpha Division for Oromocto and the south bank of the river, Charlie Division for the north bank of the river between Maugerville and Douglas Harbour, and X Division for Grand Lake.

(Above) The unofficial mayor of Maugerville Markus Harvey gives a big hug to Oromocto Fire Chief Jody Price.

(Left) Oromocto Fire Department crews help move cattle.

"Energy and Natural Resources brought in their incident-management group. They are trained for forest fires but they are learning to do all disasters. It was a forest officer from Miramichi who worked in Division X, Grand Lake. She was good," Price says. "Down in Douglas Harbour, Ken Atyeo the volunteer fire chief was a one-man show. Every day I'd send him over a crew of kids (young firefighters in their 20s) – I called them the ninjas – and they'd stay with him all day."

LONG DAYS

The Oromocto crews worked long days, delivering water to isolated people, patrolling the swollen river, offering a voice of reason and a helping hand to people in the midst of chaos.

"I told them, 'You guys are going out there today and you're the ones people will be talking about in 40 years,'" says Price, referring to the crews who worked the historic '73 flood. "But you know, I don't know if it will be another 40 years before the next one hits."

> **2,972**
> Number of damage reports/ health-and-safety inspections completed as of August 10, 2018.

Flood management always starts the same way for Price and his crews: door-to-door visits — the fire fighters call it the ground pound — to brief residents and hand out flood passes for vehicles, which will allow residents access to their homes after roads are closed to through traffic. Once the water rises too high for cars, travel is restricted to SUVs and half-tonne and then, if the water keeps rising, to three-quarter-tonne trucks. After that, it's boats only.

"Once we are into boat operations we start going around checking on people. These folks down on the river are a very resilient people; some have been there for generations," he says. "This year it got so high we started to see old timers asking to be brought out. Well, that's a different dynamic."

The length of the flood is what did most people in. Normally, people are flooded out for a few days and locals know to stock their homes with enough supplies to be self-sufficient for up to 72 hours. However, by Day 15 of the 2018 flood, Price had instructed Water Division to help people out.

"By that time, only about 30 or 40 houses out of 300 houses had people in them. Now you can't spoon feed people but at Day 15 you bend the rules. You go above and beyond because these people are trying to stay in their homes."

(Right) Walking in with supplies along Route 105 in Maugerville.

(Below) Markus Harvey (left) and David McIntyre, the latter of who has lived through a number of spring freshet and is a source of community information to emergency workers and residents.

(Left) Members of the Oromocto Fire Department and the largest Regional Emergency Operations Centre in the province. It covered 2,500 square kilometres during the flood.

1,466
Total number of power outages reported by NB Power, the provincial utility.

CATS ON PATROL

Price is proud of his crews' record this year. Across the province there were no fatalities and no major injuries. There were, however, cats. Price shakes his head and laughs. "Most injuries on the flood were cats. They were mean. We had to get the guys welding gloves."

In addition to rescuing stranded pets, the crews also assisted farmers to either relocate their cattle or move them to higher ground. For one Maugerville-area farm, the fire fighters brought over an electrician, a generator and a couple tanks of gas to keep 100 head of cattle high and dry.

It's one of the many ways flood management has changed over the years in New Brunswick.

"Back in '73 or earlier if two guys went out in a boat to save a cow and they flipped and drowned, well we'd have a funeral for them and that would be it," says Price. "I sit and talk with the old timers and they remember the way it used to be. But the world is changing, there is more emphasis on public safety and that's a very good thing."

These days, Price and his team hold regular public meetings and during the flood are made admins of the Maugerville Facebook group so they can distribute information, reply to questions and refute rumours quickly. Still, he says there's more work to be done.

He'd like to partner with a local non-profit to develop 72-hour emergency kits, such as ones purchased by the Rotary Club of Comox, British Columbia and the regional fire service. The kits are sold at half price to promote personal responsibility. When Price thinks about the increase in intensity and frequency of natural disasters in New Brunswick, he is concerned residents aren't ready for what the future holds.

"We've got to get people to be more self-sufficient. They expect the province to step in and save them," he says. "Well, the weather is going to be a lot harder on provincial resources and you can already see the province isn't going to be able to keep up with all this stuff that is happening."

(Top) Safety barriers at popular Meenans Cove beach in Quispamsis.

(Above) Crews used front-end loaders to clear water and carry sandbags.

COMMUNITY LEADERSHIP

Price says community leadership is key to building local resiliency, particularly in rural areas, which have experienced reductions in local health and safety services. "They have no ambulance in their communities, police service is less and less around, the RCMP are getting stretched thin — the only thing left in a place like Cambridge Narrows is that volunteer fire service."

Those local volunteer fire fighters could create a local emergency preparedness network that understands local needs and has the trust of the community to implement necessary changes.

"Throwing money at a problem doesn't fix the problem," says Price. "People fix the problem."

Chief Kevin Clifford subscribes to the same mantra. The head of the City of Saint John Fire Service and director of the Saint John Emergency Management Organization (SJ EMO), Clifford says disasters bring out leadership in a community.

"Those 15 days during the flood were probably some of the easiest and some of the most motivating days of our careers and part of that was watching how the community came together," he said.

"We never lost sight of the tragedy happening to people and I don't think we ever took a call that we couldn't answer. We were very empathetic to the residents' impact. Our job was to make sure their day didn't get worse, that they had confidence in us. We can't stop the wind from blowing, we can't stop the rain from falling, we just want to help our community."

MANY HAZARDS

For a small city, Saint John has one of the most diverse hazard profiles in North America. It is the only community in Canada to have both a nuclear power plant and a liquefied natural gas (LNG) terminal to consider.

It is also home to Canada's largest refinery, two major natural gas pipelines, a pulp and paper plant, rail lines, the second largest port in the Maritimes and New Brunswick's largest power generating station. All that heavy industry means city firefighters have received extensive training in how to manage chaos.

Almost immediately, Chief Clifford realized this wasn't an ordinary flood. "We were driving around and we were on the Westfield Road and we saw a trampoline floating down the river."

The city was quick to issue a voluntary evacuation order for residents in low-lying areas and to activate the SJ EMO process, which brought all 42 city services under one roof to coordinate the response.

(Left) A man carries his luggage in Darlings Island as emergency crews installed safety barriers to prevent road traffic.

SANDBAGGING IT

"We were the first to open up sandbagging stations," he says, remembering the initial conversation about the idea. "When you think about a sandbag holding back the Saint John River, it's asinine," he says, with a laugh and a shake of his head.

"It's stupid to think you can hold back that river with a sandbag. We talked about it and people doubted it would work but in the end, we did it. You know why? Because we said we are going to enable residents to help themselves even if it has no measurable impact. You know what happened. For homes right on the river's edge those sandbags made a difference."

COMING TOGETHER

It also brought the community together in a way Clifford had never witnessed before. "The story here is more about community, not the river or the flood. I'm proud that the community introduced the power of sandbagging. How else was the three-year-old and the mom and dad going to rally to help people? People felt empowered and that's good."

Throughout the flood, SJ EMO held daily public briefings in or near the communities most affected so residents could attend. It also challenged city crews to rise to the challenge of strengthening pieces of key public infrastructure in the face of a quickly moving river.

688
Number of outages still without power as of August 10, 2018.

On May 5, crews worked with Galbraith Construction to rebuild a section of Westfield Road near Mellinger Crescent to prevent residents from becoming isolated. At the same time, Saint John Water crews were designing and building a berm around the Millidgeville Wastewater Treatment Facility, which has since become a permanent addition to the site, an example of Chief Clifford's belief in building back better.

"We will continue to work harder for the next time," he says. "If you aren't aspiring to be better you are aspiring to be the same and the world is going to catch up and pass you."

Once the threat of flooding eased, SJ EMO crews went into people's homes to help them clear out water-damaged materials. Like Chief Price in Oromocto, Chief Clifford believes residents need to start developing their own strategies for dealing with natural disasters. There are four phases in emergency planning: mitigation and prevention, preparation, response and recovery. Chief Clifford suggests people use this as a guideline for figuring out what they will do when the next disaster strikes.

"When I was in the middle of this flood, I didn't have a sense of how profound it was," he says. "The Saint John River is a pretty marvellous place and is so much a fabric of this city and this province. This time the river reached out in a bad way but it also caused a lot of people to come together."

(Right) Rothesay town crews ferried equipment and sandbags to isolated residents.

(Nick Lowe cutline)

9

HELPING HANDS

(Opposite) Rob Dekany, aka Uber Rob, ferries people to and from Darlings Island.

It was the woman in chest waders carrying a baby on her shoulders that did it for Rob Dekany. "I saw that and I said, 'As if I'm going to let that happen'. So, I went right home and got my boat. I just drove around the island asking, 'Do you want a ride? Do you want a ride? Do you want a ride? and then some people said 'yeah.'"

This is how the legend of Uber Rob began.

Thirteen days; 845 trips; 4,225 passengers; 1,020 kilometres; 143 hours. Those are the numbers behind Dekany's volunteer water taxi service, which he provided to the people of Darlings Island during the 2018 flood.

With their only access road flooded, Darlings Island residents had two choices: either seek temporary shelter off the island or wade or paddle your way across the one-kilometre stretch to the mainland. Most chose to stay — the spring freshet is usually only a few days long — and soon found themselves facing a much longer period of isolation.

Then along came Dekany. The guy seemed to always be around, ready to ferry people across. Always good for a laugh, in fine spirits, happy to help.

He was, after all, a local boy, with a home on Neck Road in Quispamsis, just down river from the island. He knew those waters like the back of his hand — and as the floodwaters rose, he was happy to lend a hand too.

"I'd wake up at 5:00 and I'd be on the river from 5:30 in the morning until about 1:00 p.m. Then it would slow down a bit so I'd sleep from 1:00 to 3:00 p.m. and then I'd be out there from 3:00 until around 10:00 or 11:00."

(Left) Sandbags from The Pit in Grand Bay-Westfield.

A TRICKY PROPOSITION

(Below) Hauling sandbags in Rothesay.

He didn't see much of his own family during those first two weeks of May, but they understood. This was something he just needed to do.

"For the first five days it was just me," he says, adding Cooke Aquaculture and the Coast Guard also sent boats to help. "I had to drive through the woods and then ribbon it off so there'd be a path. There was a lot in the water. I had to avoid tractors, piles of bricks, sheds. It was tricky, especially when it became dark."

Dekany's preferred mode of transportation was a 19-foot fish and ski boat with a 150-horsepower engine. "It flies," he says.

One day he got to show it off for a special passenger. A woman in her 90s from a local seniors' home came to see him, accompanied by a healthcare aid. "She asked, 'Can you take me out to see my island?' And I said, 'Of course.'"

Dekany headed out into the swollen river and soon found himself atop the baseball diamond. "We ran the bases and then I had the boat slide home. She loved it. You gotta have fun."

When the flood finally subsided, the residents of Darlings Island threw a surprise thank you party for Dekany at the covered bridge. "The guy who nicknamed me Uber Rob said that it takes one man to bring a community together," says Dekany. "That gave me goosebumps galore."

THE PIT

The little pink scroll is tucked safely away with Brittany Merrifield's special memories. It was delivered one day by a little girl who wanted to thank all the flood helpers. It's next to the handwritten note from Robert McNutt, who wanted to thank the anonymous volunteers who had helped to save his house.

Just a typical day at the very atypical worksite known affectionately as The Pit.

It started simply enough. Brittany and her dad Bill were watching the water rush in to Grand Bay-Westfield and while neither of their homes were under threat, they felt they needed to do something to help their friends and neighbours.

Merrifield called the Hobarts, owners of Keel Construction, and asked if she, her dad and a few friends could set up a small sandbagging operation at the Hobarts' sand pit. Of course, they replied, and so on May 1 Merrifield put a note up on Facebook and a few volunteers popped by to help.

"We show up and there's this little dump of sand and we're thinking, 'That's a lot of sand.' On our first day, we filled a thousand sandbags and we were quite proud of ourselves," says Brittany, laughing at her initial naivety. "By the end we had filled 18 thousand."

The Pit, as the Grand Bay-Westfield sandbagging operation came to be known, took on a life of its own as the flood stretched into its second week. Merrifield estimates about 500 people came to volunteer and not everyone was a local.

"People drove down from Florenceville and Bathurst to help us," she says. "The woman from Bathurst lost her car keys in the sand, rented a car to get back to Bathurst to get her other set, get a key cut and then came back for her car. No, I don't know her name. Crazy."

(Above) Letter of thanks from homeowner Robert McNutt.

(Right) Cars lined the road at Darlings Island as people were forced to use water transport to reach the mainland.

THE ROLE OF SOCIAL MEDIA

Social media played a central role in bringing people together at The Pit. Armed with her mobile phone, Merrifield, who is a professional photographer, wove a story using words, images and videos of neighbours helping neighbours. That multimedia narrative attracted people to the site.

"It was a real tangible way for bringing people out. There was an 87-year-old man out there. His daughter kept saying, 'Dad that's enough,' and he kept going. People with physical disabilities, for whom sandbagging was physically difficult, came to help. They bagged," says Merrifield, shaking her head. "They were out there killing themselves to help people they didn't know and probably never will know, often with their own trucks and taking time off of work."

Throughout the week Merrifield would post on the Grand Bay-Westfield and Public Landing Facebook groups, not just to bring volunteers to the site but also to find out who needed help. Then she'd find volunteers with trucks able to deliver sandbags to homeowners. People texted, called, messaged and posted. Some needed sandbags, others needed furniture moved. The volunteers at The Pit did it all.

"Once we had it going, it became a juggernaut. Physically, it is difficult filling sandbags, and, mentally, you are dealing with exhaustion. But it was also an extremely energizing place to be. To see people coming together," says Merrifield.

"One thing that was really powerful were people whose houses were flooded came to help others. It gave you a sense of what it means to have a true vocation. There was a lot of profound meaning to this," she adds. "It didn't mean I didn't come home and have a glass of wine and two Advil at the end of the night — because I did that too."

Along the way, local businesses started making donations to the cause. Joe Foot of Quality Respiratory Care brought more than $200 worth of food. Southern Infusion Food Truck fed the volunteers for free one day. (Two days later SJ EMO hired them to feed other crews).

The local bakeshop sent stuff; so did Starbucks and Tim Hortons. Ready John dropped off port-a-potties. Irving Oil sent volunteers and a flatbed of water. Domino's and Vito's each sent pizza. Rogers sent employees; Subway sent sandwiches while Home Hardware sent shovels and trucks. The Medicine Show dropped off water and bandages while Shoppers Drug Mart sent a milk crate of sunscreen and Advil.

Starkey's Garage brought a flatbed and lift and went for days delivering sandbags. When another volunteer got a stick stuck in the radiator of his pickup while delivering sand, Starkey's fixed it for free.

"The thing about The Pit is it was a good-news story in a bad-news story. That's why people gravitated to it," says Merrifield. "Being on the river, having access to the river, it's just in us."

(Above) People found all sorts of ways to travel to and from Darlings Island in the flood waters.

2,533
Total number of people who registered with the Red Cross.

(Above) Volunteer Chris Taylor (far right) was unexpectedly thrust into leadership when she began posting on Facebook, encouraging people to volunteer in Saint John.

(Right) Maugerville's Flood Watch Community page on Facebook.

FLOOD WATCH

Everyone who used a Facebook group to stay connected during the flood owes a thank you to David Keenan. Back in 2005 he started the very first Flood Watch Facebook group for Maugerville as a way to help distribute information to family and friends in the flood zone. As a quadrapalegic, social media enables Keenan to contribute and engage with his community.

"For me, social media acts as a means of inclusion. My situation, as it is, isolates me from certain activities so with the whole realm of social media being accessible I find that inclusion becomes more tangible," he writes. "Since access to a lot of the affected areas is only limited to those in that area, what better way is there to show what's going on … I don't get over as much as I'd like so in a way I'm there without being there.

"I think there are others who are in the same boat," says Keenan. "Family members from abroad like to be kept up to date on what the spring has to offer; it's never the same way twice. Also, floods are a weather phenomenon, whether accented by human touch or not, and should be showcased."

As he describes it, the Maugerville Flood Watch page is a one-stop shop for information.

"Instead of looking and searching the Internet, the group is open and inviting to everyone and is chock full of up-to-date helpful information. I believe the group should be informative and cohesive. I was approached to do other groups for other communities but I know how time consuming this group becomes. I encouraged them to use the Maugerville Flood Watch group as a template. It comes down to being safe and informed. The more people we reach, the more knowledge we absorb."

For the first 12 years, Keenan ran the group solo. In the last few years his cousin Markus Harvey has assisted with admin duties.

"Companies, organizations, government officials all used this page to inform and/or offer services to those in the affected areas," he writes. "If this group has played a role in any way, shape or form in keeping people safe and alive than it has served its purpose."

SANDBAGGING DUTY

Abdulghani Qaba Khalil volunteered, sandbagging and cleaning up damaged properties, because he wanted to honour the people who had helped him when he and his family needed it the most. "I felt it was my duty for my community, for my Canadian brothers and sisters."

Khalil is originally from Homs, Syria, which was under siege between 2011 and 2014, a major battleground in the Syrian civil war. In 2012, Khalil and his wife Qamar Saad Aldeen were new parents and fled to Damascus in the hopes of giving their daughter a better life.

But the war followed them there and in 2013 they moved across the border to Irbid, Syria, joining the diaspora of Syrian refugees seeking safety. Along the way they welcomed their son Qusai, now five, and Farah, now three.

In 2016 they were among the first group of Syrians to move to Saint John, arriving on a bitterly cold day in January. "On my first day in Canada, in a new country, new city, new language and new culture, I saw all these Canadian people smiling at me and asking if I need anything," he says. "When I saw my Canadian brothers and sisters standing beside me it gave me such power. Such hope that I could start again."

And so he did, first by learning English and more recently by acting as a translator for other Arabic-speaking newcomers. An accountant in Syria, Khalil is taking courses and also caring for his four children — son Omram was born in 2017 — while his wife learns English at the YMCA.

When the call went out for volunteers to help with sandbagging, Khalil and about 20 of his fellow Syrian-Canadian Saint Johners answered the call. They spent the first weekend working at the Millidgeville station, the second weekend working at The Pit in Grand Bay-Westfield and the third weekend helping with cleanup activities.

"Saint John is now my city and I feel that I have a duty to help, especially when you see someone in a difficult situation."

(Above) No one was too small to help out at the sandbagging stations in Saint John.

(Left) Steve Harvey patrols Route 105 in Maugerville, part of the neighbourhood watch brigade that stayed behind to look after everyone's homes.

6,352
Total amount of debris hauled to New Brunswick landfills as of August 10, 2018.

(Above) Rob Dekany, aka Uber Rob, had to maneuver around obstacles to safely ferry people around Darlings Island.

A NEED TO HELP

Chris Taylor is motivated by a similar need to help her community. As it did to Merrifield, the flood catapulted Taylor into a community-leadership role rather unexpectedly. After her post about the generosity of the local Domino's pizza shop, the Telegraph-Journal newspaper showed up to interview her and snap her photo. That day she was sandbagging alongside fellow Irving Oil employees, all of them dressed in matching blue coveralls.

"I think people saw my photo in the paper, saw the coveralls and thought I was in charge or something," she says, laughing. "After that people just started reaching out to me."

Taylor knew some of the members of the SJ EMO because earlier in the year she had worked with them when a butane leak from the Irving Oil refinery forced the evacuation of an east-side neighbourhood. When strangers started calling Taylor, she picked up the phone and called her contact at SJ EMO.

And so began a makeshift assignment process, with the SJ EMO calling Taylor and, in turn, Taylor directing the growing number of volunteers to where they were most needed. "I was online texting and talking to people and I was going site to site. It all happened very organically."

While the widespread community participation in flood efforts was welcomed and appreciated, it was also unexpected. SJ EMO had no plan for how to coordinate its growing army of volunteers.

"The city didn't have a central place for people to call to find out what to do. There was nothing for volunteers and I get that; they were busy trying to make sure people didn't get electrocuted," says Taylor.

(Left) Volunteers of all ages work through the day filling and delivering sandbags to people in Saint John.

PEOPLE HELPING PEOPLE

Taylor went to work coordinating volunteers. She set up a sandbagging station for kids on the west side, because so many of them wanted to help. She checked on safety supplies for volunteers. She coordinated the delivery of sandbags.

"On the Sunday, I said, 'I gotta take a break,' but at 6:30 a.m. the phone started up again and I said, 'I gotta go to work.' That's what I did for five days," she says. "One day this guy — he was on his 10th load of the day — he was just done and he got down from his truck, he gives me a hug and I started crying and he started crying. I said, 'You're going to get through this,' and he said, 'Yes, we are going to get through this.' I just can't believe all these people.'"

Neither could Blair and Rosalyn Hyslop, the new owners of Kredl's Country Market. They had purchased the Hampton landmark in December 2017 and were just preparing the greenhouses and cookhouse for their first spring season when the flood warning was issued.

The Hyslops, who also own Mrs. Dunster's, were told water rarely flooded the market. To be on the safe side, they and some of their employees built a three-foot wall of sandbags around the greenhouse.

(Above) Books, food, furniture and plants were all placed on countertops and shelves at Erika Betts and Mike Derrah home.

Then Blair got in the truck and drove to Miramichi to go fishing. "I thought the sandbags were a bit of overkill but we were prepared," he says.

Three hours later, as he pulled into Miramichi, Rosalyn called: the water was 2.5-feet (.75-metres) high. Blair turned the truck around and rushed back to Hampton.

When four inches of water appeared in the cookhouse, the Hyslops knew they were in trouble. Then Blair put a call out on Facebook for pumps. "Then this amazing thing happened. All these people showed up with pumps. They'd drop them off and then leave. People we didn't know."

Even with 10 borrowed pumps, the cookhouse was still in danger. "A couple of us started talking about putting sandbags all around the cookhouse but it was such a monumental task, people were cynical, they didn't believe it could be done. But I said, let's try and see what happens."

Less than three hours, and four thousand sandbags, later, the cookhouse was secured. "Dozens and dozens of people showed up. The operation was incredible. As we kept extending the line of sandbags, more and more people would show up."

SHOWING THANKS

In gratitude, the Hyslops and Kredl's staff made lunch for all the volunteers, who ate and then promptly got to work cleaning up all the flood debris.

"Dan Coleman, he's a landscaper, he shows up with two trucks and a tractor. For the next six hours people cleaned up debris. Dan took 20 trucks of debris away. It looked a bit surreal, standing on this nice clean pavement next to a wall of sandbags and three feet of water."

ALL THAT IN A DAY

As Hyslop sat behind his community-built wall of sand, he had time to watch the people of Hampton. The bridge near Kredl's had been closed to traffic as the Hampton River rose to sit level with it. This meant people had to walk across it.

"I'd sit out front and watch blue-collar guys walking back and forth with lunch pails. Nurses. Parents with their kids and backpacks. You could sit there at the market and see people trying to go on with their own lives," said Hyslop. "It was a different experience and so that day I wrote a Facebook post to sincerely thank everybody."

Blair posted it and didn't think about it again. The next day he woke to his phone buzzing with requests from media across the country. His post had gone viral.

"What the flood did was it restored people's pride in the place. They literally grabbed Roslyn and I by the arm and said, 'Welcome.' That flood, if there is a silver lining in this, is that it gave Kredl's back to the community."

(Above) The main road through Robertson Point was reduced to dirt and gravel by the pounding waves and strong currents of Grand Lake.

10

BUILD BACK BETTER

(Opposite) Marian and Bruce Langhus are renovating their bed and breakfast in Gagetown using natural wood and mould-proof insulation.

Marian and Bruce Langhus will tell you all about the day the 2018 flood came to town, but if you really want to get them chatting, ask them what insulation they use.

"It's made of basalt rock. It's heated up and it becomes like grey cotton candy," says Marian Langhus of their Rockwool Insulation. "It will not hold mould." This makes the Langhuses very happy. Looking around the remains of their sitting room, it's easy to understand why.

They own and operate Lang House Bed and Breakfast on Gagetown's main street. It was built in 1880 by a riverboat captain and in the mid-20th century it was owned by a nurse, who was also the local midwife. She turned the front room into the birth room and helped deliver 183 babies; Marian was baby number 43.

"We bought in 2015 and that first year the basement flooded. Then in 2017 water splashed in. After this year, we said, 'Okay, let's plan.'"

The 2018 flood was not kind to Lang House. It roared in, filling the basement, and the water was knee deep on the first floor, including the kitchen, hallways and the aforementioned sitting room, which boasts a beautiful view of the river.

"We evacuated April 27," says Marian. "That night, Bruce had stayed up trying to pump the basement but the river came over the banks. When the water rose, it was so fast. Bruce lay down for a nap and during that time I realized it was going to come in. I looked at him and said, 'I've got news: we're leaving.'"

(Left) Lang House B&B in Gagetown became a construction site after the flood destroyed the first floor.

DEAD FISH FLOATING

When they returned, after the water had subsided, their pressed-wood floors had buckled, there were burn marks around an electrical socket and dead fish were floating in the basement.

"The biggest race was to get ahead of the mould. We filled two dumpsters of heavy wet bags that went to the landfill."

The Langhuses are retired geologists and knew if they were going to continue to operate the B&B they had to figure out a way to live with the river, rather than fight against it.

They applied for $60,000 in disaster relief and, like many others in the flood zone, were frustrated by the slowness of the claims process and the lack of information, particularly advice on how to rebuild with better, more flood-resistant materials.

For the Langhuses, that meant no more pressed wood. They ripped up all the flooring, going back to the original narrow, hardwood boards. "The flooring does dry eventually."

They've moved the oil tank around to the back of the house, to a high point in the front yard. All the electrical sockets and phone jacks are being reinstalled halfway up the wall, above the flood line. They're creating new storage spaces on the first and second floors.

"My hope is people give themselves the flexibility to do things smart," says Marian.

(Above) Contractor Doug Ryan (left) and Tyler Thomas of Phoenix Overhaul Solutions are helping to make Lang House B&B more flood resistant.

(Above) In some areas, such as Grand Lake, the cleanup was extensive.

(Right) Before and after shot of Mark Ellis' cottage. He had it lifted it prior to 2018 but that wasn't enough to keep the flood waters away.

RACING THE WATER

Carol and Francis Hebert are learning as they go. After the 2008 flood, they raised their house on the Nerepis Road, built a basement and installed a sump pump. The following year, as the water raced in, they slept at low tide and woke with the high tide, sweeping water towards the pump.

They have all their plugs high on the walls, the plugs in the barn come down from the ceiling and their furnace hangs on joists. The greenhouse, garage and barn are all on individual breakers.

Now, following this latest flood, Hebert is installing pine-board flooring and using marina varnish. "I figure if it keeps a boat dry . . ." she says with a chuckle. "Before the flood, I had been saying I wanted to declutter. Well, maybe not this much but the house did get decluttered. Mother Nature teaches us lessons; she's real good at it."

Greg MacCallum of the NB EMO says people will need to develop strategies for dealing with an increasing number of intense weather events. "Preparedness isn't just government's job. We will do more education but things aren't going to improve from a climatology point of view," he says. "People are going to have to be more resilient than they have been in the past."

David Keenan, who runs the Maugerville Flood Watch Facebook group, says EMO needs to do more to build trust in communities before the next disaster hits. "Experience counts. EMO likes facts and figures. I'd sooner listen to [Markus] Harvey who lives at 'ground zero' than to someone who visits 'ground zero' when and if necessary. There is a wealth of knowledge that comes from living," writes Keenan.

"Tension is EMO's enemy, and they seem to show up when it's at its peak. We live a defensive existence and are quick to play the blame game. EMO takes that blow and it has not gained any popularity this year; their planning strategy seems to be on the fly, which is not very practical.

"My Mom woke my brother and nephew screaming because she woke to use the washroom and stepped in water, electricity still on, and it's a wonder they never got electrocuted."

(Mark Ellis photo)

(Left) One Grand Lake area cottage, ready for the landfill.

> **2 DEGREES C TO 4 DEGREES C**
> Average rise in summer temperatures expected by 2050. Winter temperatures are expected to rise by 2 degrees C by 2050.

TIGHTLY-KNIT COMMUNITIES

"Our family has never seen the water rise this fast," writes Keenan, "For the most part we are prepared; 44 years living in a flood zone you learn. Small communities are tightly knit and members do step up, you can put stock in that. Maybe EMO can learn something there."

It's not just geographic communities that can provide new perspectives to emergency management. Bernie Connors found his community in CivicTech, a Fredericton-based volunteer organization that develops technical solutions to social issues.

A career civil servant, Connors had been wanting to create a mobile version of the government's popular River Watch website since March 2010, but he could never find a team of people who wanted to take it on.

"The premise was, what good is an app if you're flooded out of your home and don't have access to your home computer?"

He sketched out a design in PowerPoint in 2014 and in 2015 pitched it at one of Planet Hatch's hackathons, at which people vote on the projects they'd like to try and solve. No one voted for Connors' mobile flood-watch app.

Then, in October 2017, he read about a new organization called CivicTech and decided to try again. "Organizer Sandi MacKinnon was just wrapping up and I said, 'If you have some time I've got a project to pitch right now.'"

The group were keen and two weeks later they got to work at The Ville, a co-location space on Fredericton's north side.

"We made a list," explains Connors. "The must-haves and the easy-to-dos went into version one. The nice to-haves and the hard-to-dos we saved for future versions. Getting together to work on this, from whiteboard to mobile app, supported on a government server, is more than I could have expected."

DIGITAL TOOLS

Brazilian Richardo Nicolini of CivicTech says working on the app helped connect him with his new home in a meaningful way.

"Other people with traditional skills, such as carpentry, are able to use their skills to help their community, but what can us geeks do?" says Nicolini. "CivicTech allows us to use our technical skills to help our community, to give back to our community."

The app launched March 21, 2018 — the first day of spring and just in time for the 2018 flood. By the end of July the River Watch mobile app had recorded 55,454 page views and 44, 543 unique views.

In the past six years, New Brunswick has experienced eight climate-related extreme-weather events, all caused by fresh water. There was flooding and evacuations in Perth-Andover and St. Stephen in 2012 and 2013. Freezing rain disrupted services in the lower Saint John River Valley in December 2013.

(Above) The Kennebecasis River floods out a low-lying road near Darlings Island.

(Steve Dionne photo)

(Right) Debris floats in the flood waters in the Grand Lake region.

(Ken Redmond photo)

(Left) Carol Hebert was grateful for the help she received from the volunteers of Christian Aid Ministries, which was one of several faith-based organizations to help homeowners clear out destroyed basements and homes.

Post-tropical storm Arthur caused widespread damage and power outages in 2014. More than 125 mm of rain caused a severe precipitation event that washed out roads, culverts and bridges across the province in September 2015. A record snowfall in Saint John brought 470 centimetres to the city in 2015. The ice storm in the Acadian Peninsula caused widespread outages in 2017. And now, heavy rains up north exacerbated the 2018 spring flood.

Digital tools that put information directly in the hands of the people who need it will be increasingly important to help navigate natural disasters, including floods.

ADAPTING TO CHANGE

The increasing frequency of these extreme-weather events prompted New Brunswick Auditor General Kim MacPherson to conduct a performance audit of the province's climate-change-adaptation plans in 2017. In 2018 she participated in a joint review by all of Canada's auditor generals.

Overall, New Brunswick is heading in the right direction. It ranks somewhere in the middle of the pack for adaptation and it is one of eight provinces with an actual plan in place. The next step, says MacPherson, is to prioritize the actions, identify which departments of government are responsible and establish a timeline for completion.

"The government should also legislate some things because that shows the government of the day is serious about tackling this issue," she says. "Generally speaking, temperatures are rising and in Canada, temperatures are rising two to three times faster than the global average."

MacPherson used to work in the budget office of the Department of Finance and she remembers a time when applying for federal disaster assistance was something that happened every few years. "Now it's routine," she says. "We do know the frequency and intensity of weather events is increasing, which means we need mitigation strategies."

SAINT JOHN RIVER
The Saint John River supports the greatest diversity of freshwater animals and fish in the Atlantic Maritime Ecozone, which includes New Brunswick, Prince Edward Island, Nova Scotia and the Gaspé Peninsula.

(Above) Rothesay residents row and wade through their flooded road near the Kennebecasis River.

(Right) Wading through flood waters.

(Far Right) Michelle Cain looks for belongings in debris from homes and cottages destroyed by the floodwater from the Saint John River in Robertson's Point, N.B.

HISTORIC FLOOD

Mike Carr thinks about mitigation a lot. His position, as manager of the Saint John EMO, was created following tropical storm Arthur. He was newly installed when Snowmageddon hit in 2015. Since then he's dealt with flash floods in the city's east side and now a historic river flood.

"We need policy changes on land use. We have to pay attention to climate change and climate-change adaptation."

That means being prepared to bring as much expertise as possible to the decision-making table. He argues that process is best administered through the EMO system.

"There is a hesitation to hit the EMO button. Why? EMO is a collaboration of all the resources you have in your community," he says. "If I run out of resources, I just ask the province and they get it for me. And when they run out, they ask the feds. That's how it's supposed to work."

There is one other crucial resource that Carr believes is essential as New Brunswick begins to figure out how to live with climate change: ordinary residents.

During the 2018 flood, New Brunswickers came to the aid of both neighbours and strangers at a level that surprised officials.

"Now that we've done it, I guarantee we'll have double the number of people next time," says Carr. "People will expect us to open up and we absolutely should. We have this really awesome resource called the community. How do we utilize it better? This is the only way we are going to have an effective response to the next flood.

"It has to be with the community."

11

COMMUNITIES ON THE RISE

(Opposite) Wolastoqiyik visual artist Natalie Sappier's Fishing on the Wolastoq.

Grand Chief of Wolastoq Ron Tremblay is experiencing something that only a short while ago he hadn't thought possible: hope.

"There was a time I didn't believe in that word but in recent years I've seen how our young people are waking up. They are starving for knowledge and wisdom."

After a lifetime of advocating for the Wolastoqiyik and for the central role the Wolastoq River plays in the lives and culture of the people who live along its banks, Tremblay is looking to the next generation to chart a new path forward.

He describes these young people as two-eye seeing, a term introduced to Tremblay by Mi'kmaw Elder Albert Marshall. It means seeing the strengths of Indigenous knowledge through one eye and the strengths of Western knowledge through the other.

"I do have hope in our young people," Tremblay says. "We need to stop asking permission and just get out there and do it. That is what they are doing."

THE WATER SPIRIT

Visual artist and storyteller Natalie Sappier credits Tremblay as one of the people who has helped her deepen her connection with the Wolastoq River and further develop her way of seeing.

(Markus Harvey photo)

(ACAP photo)

(Above) Graeme Stewart Robertson of the Atlantic Coastal Action Program (ACAP) Saint John is part of a growing movement of community-based non-profits that are helping local residents better understand their part of the river system and how they can become more water considerate.

(Left) Maugerville community barbeque to bring people together after the flood.

Her Wolastoqiyik name is Samagani Cocahq, which means The Water Spirit. She grew up in Tobique First Nation and used to swim in the river as a teenager. But as she got older she lost her connection to the river.

"I think the stories that were in me came out when I participated in my first traditional ceremony," she says. "It is a very spiritual place I go to through my art. My teachings are from the land and from the water. That is the gift I have been given, to share my journey in any form that I can."

For Sappier, the way forward will always involve the river. "That's where we live, that's where the ancestors are. Water wakes me. It wakes the song I need to hear, it grounds me and it gives me purpose," she says, as she sits in her favourite Fredericton coffee shop, a stone's throw from the riverbank. "We need to consider how we are going to take care of this river, which is in our name."

Downriver in Saint John, Graeme Stewart Robertson is sitting outside watching the activity at the mouth of the river. Turbines for the Bay of Fundy tidal energy site sit at Long Wharf, a container ship sits on the west side and tourists walk along Harbour Passage.

As the executive director of the Atlantic Coastal Action Program (ACAP) Saint John, Stewart-Robertson spends his days seeking community-based solutions to watershed management in arguably one of the most unusual local ecosystems in the world.

"The Saint John Harbour is probably one of the least appreciated parts of the Saint John River," he says. "It's the interplay of tide and river, salt and freshwater, rainwater and melt water, and it all comes to a head in the greater Saint John area. It is something we should be proud of."

(Above) Submerged vehicles and flooded garages were a common sight in the Grand Lake-Maugerville-Sheffield area.

(Right) Grand Chief of Wolastoq Ron Tremblay took this photo of the river, the rain and the sunset. It reminds him of the strength and beauty of the river.

A WATERSHED MOMENT

Stewart-Robertson describes the 2018 flood as a watershed moment for the city and the province. He's taking calls from residents interested in flood-risk mapping. They hope to better understand their neighbourhoods and how to be more prepared for the next flood.

City staff are beginning to see climate adaptation as a means to solving other challenges, such as creating more green spaces and treed areas along the river to mitigate against future floods, and to create recreational spaces to lower social isolation and improve the health of city residents.

"Almost every New Brunswicker has a relationship with water but one of the biggest challenges people have is a complete misunderstanding of what it means to be a steward of it," he says. "We need to become water considerate. We are very used to it on our coasts but not on our river systems. This could be a potential proving ground for ideas."

Back in Douglas Harbour, Eldon Hunter rings through another order of ice, chips and a ticket for that night's lottery. He waves a friendly hello to a few contractors, rings in another order of gas and leans back against the cash register and smiles.

"Look, people that are here love it; they love summers here and it's been going on for 200 years. Yes, there are a lot of tears right now but at the end of the day we are going to go where we love to be.

So, we are going to do what we can to get it back."